LUCKY HOUSE NUMBERS

YOUR HOUSE NUMBER HOLDS THE KEY

DONNA STELLHORN

© 2023 ETC Publishing

www.etcpublishing.com

ISBN: 978-1944622220

Table of Contents

Why House Numbers?

"Is my house number lucky?" I find this question often in comments on my YouTube channel and in my email inbox. What they are asking me is, "Is this home a good choice for my family and me?"

That's an important question, one almost all of us have asked ourselves at some point or another. Determining whether a home is right for us is a complex matter with several factors to consider, such as layout, location, style, size, and most importantly, the "feel" of the home. It's the energy or the "feel" that we're going to talk about in this book about house numbers.

It has always mystified me that after a quick walkthrough of an apartment or house, we're supposed to make a massive decision about where we're going to live for the next year, five years, ten years, or the rest of our lives. Frankly, there have been instances when I've taken more time to pick out a pair of shoes than to choose a home. That's why so many people write me panicked emails and texts—often after signing on the dotted line—asking, "did I choose the best home for my family?"

Because of how much effort it takes to move, it's impossible to "try out" a home. We need other criteria to determine whether a home will be good for us. Factors like size, location, neighborhood, yard, access to schools, proximity to shopping, reliable internet, away from indus-trial areas, close to work, etc., all play a role. You can get all these right and still not feel at home because the house itself has a "feeling," an energy signature that's unique to that house or apartment. This book is about understand-ing the energy of a house or apartment through the number. Moreover, if you discover that you and your family are not in harmony with that energy, we will explore techniques to shift the energy and create a happy, healthy, and prosperous home.

But why does the number reveal the energy of a house or apartment?

First, let's define what we mean by "energy" Everything in the Universe is made up of tiny little gyrating particles. These particles are vibrating at various frequencies. When we say that something has "an energy," we're refer-ring to its vibration.

The names we give things help describe the vibration or energy. My apologies to Shakespeare, but studies show a rose by any other name may NOT smell as sweet if, for instance, that name was "thorny blub bush." The whole "science" of branding is based on the concept that you can sell anything if you find the right name to label it. Remember Pet Rocks? I had one as a kid. It was a rock. I bought a rock, and it became a pet because it was called a Pet Rock.

Names have a particular vibration. You have a name. Your name is probably listed in one or more official government documents in the country you live in or were born in. Your name is used to help verify who you are, and more importantly, the world finds you primarily through your name. There's a connection between your energy and the energy of your name.

If you were to change your name, your new name's vibration would affect your life. Many people know this and go through the legal process to change their first name. Women experience this when they take their husband's surname. Young adults feel this when they throw off a childhood nickname and ask people to call them by their given name.

*THE NUMBER OF YOUR HOME OR
APARTMENT IS ITS NAME.*

It's the same with a home. A house gets an address, usually assigned through some official agency, which makes the house find-able. The world can locate the home through its address.

Like your own name, the number of your home has a vibration, an energy, a "feeling." The energy of a house number affects both the home and those who live there. You may have already experienced this. In one house, you may have found an excellent income came effortlessly, yet in another you have trouble paying the bills. In one house, you may have been able to keep the house clean and tidy, and another house seems to get messy all by itself.

A home's energy affects your energy, emotions, and how you relate to others within the house and those outside your home. The vibration/ energy of a home affects your ability to take on the world, find a suitable job, accumulate money, feel motivated to start a business, and more. The energy of the home affects how you are at home and in the world.

Often we're attracted to energies vibrating at the same frequency as our own. If you're feeling very independent, courageous, and stubbornly refusing to ask for help from anyone, you are most likely drawn to houses having an intense ONE energy (the house number is a ONE, or there are many ONEs in the number or the number itself adds up to ONE).

Having this energy in your life can be fine and even helpful, but two problems can occur. You can move into the house, get settled, then decide you want to get into a relationship—but the vibration of the house brings only opportunities to remain single. Or your family moves into this house, and each person takes on a very independent energy. You feel less connected as a family. Everyone does their own thing, and you struggle to bring the family back together.

Energy cannot be created or destroyed, but it can shift in form. It's very difficult to change a house number (without some considerable legal expense.) However, you *can* shift the energy to find a beneficial use for it, **even with so-called unlucky numbers**. This is the essence of Feng Shui. Change your environment, and the energy will shift.

House Number versus Street Address

So why not consider the full street address to determine the energy of a home? We can and should look at the entire address; however, the house number itself is of prime importance. Continuing the analogy of the address being a name, the street name is the surname, as all the houses on the street share the street name. So the number and street together are like a person's first name and family name. The house number or apartment number alone conveys the energy of the individual house or apartment unit.

THE HOUSE NUMBER AND THE ROOT NUMBER

When working with a house number's energy, we consider the number and then reduce the number down to its root number. These two numbers, the full house number and the root number are equally important. House numbers between 1 and 9 have only a root number. So if you live at 5 Pleasant Circle, your house number and your root number are FIVE.

Most house numbers have several digits. For example, while the root number of two houses, 1215 and 972, are both NINE, the house numbers are entirely different. House number 1215 is about independent people coming together with a united purpose creating change, adventure, and opportunity resulting in long-term happiness and success. 972 is about thoughtful people living by intention and their own beliefs, creating meaningful relationships and work/life balance resulting in long-term happiness and success. In this book, we'll be discussing the energy of the root numbers and how to apply that meaning to the whole house number. I won't be able to cover the meaning of every possible house number in this book, but you connect with me to get information about specific house numbers on my website, https://DonnaStellhorn.com/

How to Find the Root Number.

Finding the root number is done by simply adding the digits together until you reach a number between 1 and 9. For example, if your house number is 1234, we find the root number by adding the numbers together and keep adding until we have a single digit. So 1+2+3+4 = 10, 1+0=1.

IF YOU WANT TO FIND THE ROOT NUMBER OF AN ENTIRE ADDRESS

As mentioned before, the energy of your particular home is in the house number or apartment number. But it's still useful and interesting to look at the whole address. This will give you information about how the house will be in the neighborhood. Is this the house that will be the one children play at? Will this be the house that is broken into? Will this be the house that sells quickly for a profit?

To find the root number of the entire address, we convert any letters in the address to numbers. Each letter corresponds to its numerical position in the alphabet. So A = 1, B = 2, and so on to Z = 8 (Z is the 26th letter of the alphabet and 2+6=8). If the language where your home is located has more letters or fewer letters in its alphabet, then your numbers will change accordingly. For example, the Russian alphabet has 32 letters. However, if the language of the country where you're living doesn't have an alphabet (such as Japan) and the language has characters instead, then use the numbers only.

For this book, we're going to be focusing on the house number itself.

WHAT IF MY HOUSE OR APARTMENT NUMBER IS NOT ORDINARY?

In some cases, there's confusion about the house or apartment number because of letters or special characters.

House or Apartment numbers that include letters: If the number includes a letter, such as 123A, we consider the letter as part of the house or apartment number. Convert the letter to a number, A=1, B=2, and so on. So, in this case, 123A is like 1231. Another example would be apartment number L6. This would be 126 as L is the twelfth letter of the alphabet. To find the root number, we would add 1+2+6 = 9. So the dwelling L6 is a 126 with a root number of 9.

Apartment numbers that include building numbers: If the number on the door of an apartment has both the unit and the building number, such as 83-123, then we take into account the whole number. If, however, you live in building 83 but on your door is 123, then we only consider the number 123.

When there's a difference between what's on the door and the postal address: Sometimes what's on the door doesn't match the mailing address. A mailing address may contain a building number or, in rare cases, be entirely different from the number on the door. As long as official government agencies deliver to either address, you will feel the energy of the number on the door.

If the post office delivers your mail to a different number than is on your door, you may have to consider both numbers. Calculate each root number separately.

Occasionally there will be a second number based on the number assigned before the house was built, like a "lot number." For example, where I live now has a 27 on the door, and its postal address is 27, but on real estate records, it's listed as Lot 46. When the unit was advertised for rent, it was listed both as number 27 and number 46. In this home, I have experienced the energy of NINE (2+7) and have not felt the energy of ONE (4+6). The vibration of the home that's strongest is based on the number on the door.

Can We Just Change the Number on the Door?

It's not effective to just put a different number on your house to get better energy. If you need to change a house's energy by changing the number, consider going through local city or county channels to change the house number officially. This would include changing the postal address, real estate records, and the number displayed on the house itself. *Note: this book is about describing the energy of a residence and, if necessary, shifting the energy without going through the legal hassles of trying to get the number changed.*

In the case of an empty lot: For people who own land without a house on it, there is a lot number to consider. A lot number is not usually the same as a house number. The lot number expresses the lot's energy and how the construction will go, but it won't tell you the energy of the house itself. Only when the city/county/government assigns the house number, will you know the home's energy. If you can choose the house number, consider the choice carefully. You can contact me through my website at https://DonnaStellhorn.com/

Now we'll discuss the energy of each root number. If you find yourself in a home with an "unlucky" number or just in energy you're not happy with, you can take steps to shift the energy. We'll talk about how to do this.

The Meaning of Numbers

"The numbers of Pythagoras were hieroglyphic symbols, by means whereof he explained all ideas concerning the nature of things," Porphyry, philosopher, c. 300 A.D.

People have been reading the meaning in numbers for as long as they've been counting. From the ancient Chaldeans to the Egyptians to the Greeks to the Hebrews, civilization after civilization looked at numbers and saw meaning.

Today the study of numerology grows and is added to by teachers and professionals. And as we add more numbers into our lives with phone numbers, passwords, license plates, and of course, house numbers, the meaning of numbers becomes more significant. We feel the vibration of the energy of numbers throughout our lives.

Universal Versus Cultural Meaning of Numbers

Numbers have universal meanings, but they can also have cultural meanings. We should consider these nuanced meanings. For example, in the United States, the number SEVEN is often viewed as lucky; for one reason, it rhymes with the word "heaven" (see more in the section on SEVEN). But in Asian countries, the number 7 is considered less lucky (though not wholly unlucky). The seventh month of the Chinese calendar is called 'the Ghost Month.' During this month, the veil between the living and dead is open, and ghosts are permitted to visit the living realm. This is just one of the reasons that some have negative feelings towards the number SEVEN.

When you are interpreting numbers, first consider the Universal meaning and how that applies to your situation. Then add any culturally specific influences. This book focuses on my own experiences of how we view numbers here in the United States and how they are felt in Feng Shui, the Chinese perspective. If you have information about number meanings from other cultures, I would love to hear about it. You can write to me through my website at https:// DonnaStellhorn.com/

Fun Exercise: How Numbers are Written has Meaning Also.

Before you read further, take a sheet of paper, and write numbers 1 through 9. Write them large, writing them in one column down the page. Set the list aside for now. As you read the meaning of each written number, compare it to how you've written your list of numbers.

1 2 3 4 5 6 7 8 9

The Meaning of Written Numbers
(INCLUDING THE FONT OF NUMBERS
ON YOUR HOME)

With written numbers, the number has an upper, middle, and lower zone. You may remember this from early school when you had to practice your letters and numbers on large, lined paper. Each of these zones has meaning.

The base or bottom third of the written number represents earth, the physical and material portions of our lives. Emphasis in this area brings more attention to physical activity, money matters, and material goods in the home.

The upper part or the top third of the written number is about our spiritual and intellectual aspects. When this part is highlighted, there's more focus on intellectual matters, religion, speaking, writing, and study.

Then there is the middle part that either connects these two aspects—earth and spirit—or keeps them separate. When the interesting bits of the written number or the font are in this middle area, there's an emphasis on work/life balance and connecting the mundane to a higher purpose.

There is m happen ore about this as we continue into the detailed interpretation of each of the nine root numbers.

Interpreting the Numbers
and How to Shift the Energy.

ONE

*THE NUMBER OF BEGINNINGS, SELF-RELIANCE,
AND SUCCESSFULLY GOING IT ALONE*

All things need a beginning, and they begin with ONE. It is the genesis. The energy of number ONE is about being first, relying on yourself alone, and taking action. The special power of ONE is it can be divided into any number, leaving both numbers unchanged. Its energy can interact with other energies and be unchanged itself. ONE is whole and complete on its own. This is a "live and let live" attitude.

But it also means it doesn't necessarily have the power to change other energies (not that we can change another person). ONE is a leader, but others must choose to follow. The ONE energy doesn't have the power to influence like some other number energies have.

The number ONE represents pioneers, explorers, and innovators. This could be the person tinkering away in their workshop and emerging with an invention that helps the world. This could be the president of an organization or CEO. This could be the person who travels the world and has many exciting experiences. The energy has tenacity, especially when there is a risk of coming in second. ONE stands as an authority, leading the way. It is a dynamic, decisive action taker.

You might find living in this house gives you:

- A strong desire to lead or be first or put in charge of something, such as a group, team, or organization.

- A desire to explore things you haven't done before and places you haven't been before.

- An ability to take quick action and get more done.

- An interest and/or need to take care of your physical self.

Too Much ONE Energy: Sometimes the energy becomes out of balance, and there's too much ONE energy. This can happen because the home's outward appearance is the same as the root number, such as a ONE home with iron bars, windows, fences with sharp points, or 'no trespassing' signs. Or it can be because your name or birth number also has a strong connection to the energy of ONE. For example, the first name Aaron (the letter A has the energy of ONE), or someone born on January 11, would already have so much ONE energy in their life that a ONE house could give them so much ONE energy it puts them out of balance. The challenge is that with so much personal ONE energy, the individual can be naturally drawn to a ONE house.

If the energy of this number is too strong, you may find yourself:

- Uncharacteristically obstinate.

- Overly self-reliant and unable to see the value of being in a relationship.

- Unable to find a suitable love relationship or only attract people who are not interested in a relationship.

- Quick to anger, even to the point of aggression or fighting.

CULTURAL MEANING

In the West, we put great emphasis on the power of being number ONE. You stand on your own two feet, and you rely on no one but yourself. The image of the "self-made man" is almost mythical in the United States. We are encouraged from our youth to be independent and self-reliant. If you are looking for this energy, a ONE house is a perfect choice for you.

The number ONE can be regarded as unlucky in cultures that value the dual concept of Yin and Yang, but more often, ONE is seen as powerful and invulnerable. It's represented by the Water element. While the ONE stands alone, it can begin a new connection at any moment.

The house number is 10
The energy is ONE (1+0=1).

The ONE energy is
increased by the strong
vertical lines

The ONE energy is
emphasized by the single
straight path to the door.

Too much ONE energy can cause problems with existing
relationships or block new relationships. Consider changing
the front walkway to add a curve. Also add a couple of large
trees to the front yard. And perhaps soften some of the
vertical lines with the addition of awnings over windows.

IF YOU WANT MORE ONE ENERGY:

There is a lot of positive energy in the number ONE and yet I have never heard anyone say their lucky number was ONE in all my years. To add more ONE energy to your home to get the benefits of the ONE energy:

- Have a single large tree or a large single potted plant on the porch.

- Add iron bars or a decorative iron fence with strong vertical lines and sharp points.

- Have a wishing well, small bridge, old wagon, or other large singular decorative piece on the front lawn.

- Inside, have a picture or statue of a solitary person or object in your entryway or by the front door, like a landscape painting of a single tree.

IF YOU WANT LESS ONE ENERGY:

- Have multiple potted plants on the porch or along the walkway.

- Avoid highlighting any single architectural feature of the house; instead, have pairs or multiples of the same feature.

- Make sure there's more than one chair on the front porch.

- Have artwork inside near the front door with many elements in it, for example, an ocean scene with many boats or a forest with many trees.

HOW ONE IS WRITTEN

It used to be that the number ONE was written as a single horizontal line. We still see this in China. Over the years, that line changed directions and became vertical. ONE can be written in two ways. It can be a vertical line, simple and straight, or it can have a serif (a semi-structural detail at the end of a stroke), in this case, a vertical line making a little "hat" and a horizontal line making a big base or "foot."

Take a look at how you wrote your number ONE, or the font used on your house or apartment number. If you made the simple vertical line, it suggests you are a straightforward individual who focuses on one thing at a time. You are a person who wants just the facts, no fluff. You want the quickest route home or the most efficient way to do something. And you want the opportunity to do it yourself, whatever it is.

Or did you add the top and base to the number, giving it added stability and flair? The serif-ed ONE says you want to be noticed for your individuality and leadership, and the solid footing shows an unwavering conviction of your authority.

THE HOUSE NUMBER FONT OF ONE

Notice the font and style of the house number painted on or attached to your home. An unadorned ONE signals you will take much action when living in the house. You will look for efficient ways of doing things. Self-sufficiency will be vital to you, so you may have an emergency kit, cook at home, or have a workshop. If your house number's font has the serif, when living in the house you speak with authority. You will make decisions more quickly and with more certainty.

EXAMPLES OF ONE HOUSES:

1: If you live in a single-family home with house number 1, the house is probably situated on a corner, bringing its own set of problems. A house on a corner is more vulnerable, as one side is not 'watched over' by a neighboring house. There can be much more street noise, and headlights may shine into the house from turning cars. Feng Shui cures can remedy these issues. These issues aside, this house number can be beneficial to a person wanting their own business, who is happily single, or is moving out on their own for the first time and learning to be independent.

10: This is the number of creation, a combination of the male phallic symbol ONE and female womb symbol ZERO, the two energies from which all things come. This is a lucky number in many ways. Often we think of things being increased by 10, such as an order of magnitude.

Most countries count their money by tens. In this house, you can add to the family through birth or marriage, create a business, or a couple can have a fulfilling intimate life.

100: In Feng Shui, this number means longevity. This home will bring energy that encourages the residents to live healthful, full lives through their positive actions.

1000: This number means "very much" or "forever" in Feng Shui terms. It would be wise to make sure you are happy with what you have in this house because you will have it for a while. This could include your partner, your job, and your stuff. This number brings energy of abundance that lasts.

TWO

THE NUMBER OF PARTNERSHIPS, BALANCE, AND HARMONY

The number TWO is about polarities, opposites coming together to benefit each other. TWO represents couples and relationships. TWO is a softer number (but not weaker energy), denoting the more passive energy of cooperation and understanding. This energy is about following a lead or making a joint decision, living in harmony, and finding balance.

Because this energy is about balance, there's a great desire to have a balanced work/life. Experiences, especially shared experiences, will be sought over just accumulating material things.

When a person is alone or choosing to be single, they can live in this house but may find a lot of outside pressure to find a partner. With this energy, partnerships can be established with a pet or deep relationship with a child or a friend.

When you live in this energy, there can be the challenge of feeling you never have time to yourself. You might find there is always someone around or that boundaries within the house are hard to maintain. You tried to tell people "knock before entering" but others may not listen.

Multiplying any number by the number TWO doubles it, and so it is the same with the energy of TWO. It increases what it touches two-fold. So this energy aids in increasing abundance and creating harmony.

You might find living in this house gives you:

- A desire to spend more time with your partner or an intense attachment to a pet or child.

- A strong need to be in a relationship and opportunities to find a great partner.

- Opportunities to connect with others, including neighbors, on a deeper level.

- A desire for work/life balance.

Too Much TWO Energy: Sometimes the energy becomes out of balance, and there's too much TWO energy. This can happen when the outward appearance of the home mirrors the vibration of the number, such as a TWO home with matching trees on either side of the house, a center-entrance home with the same number of windows on either side of the door, a pair of columns holding up a portico or all the lawn art and plantings in perfect pairs. It can also be because your name or birth number has a strong connection to the energy of TWO. For example, the first name Betty (the letters B and T have the energy of TWO.) Someone born on February 22 would already have so much TWO energy in their life that a TWO house could put them out of balance. The challenge is that with so much TWO energy the person has personally, they will be naturally attracted to a TWO house.

- If the energy of this number is too strong, you may find yourself:

- Having a strong need for reassurance from others about decisions you need to make.

- Feeling like it's hard to be alone, that you always want people around.

- Having a desire to stay in a bad relationship so that you don't have to look for someone new or you won't have to be alone.

- Feeling too passive, waiting for others to take the lead.

CULTURAL MEANING

In the West, the number TWO has a very similar meaning to its universal meaning.

In the East, it's a different story. In Feng Shui, all even numbers are Yin numbers (yielding and passive), but the number TWO represents the duality of Yin and Yang, the opposing energies coming together, the two sides of one coin. It means that one side cannot exist without the other. When there are two sides, there is peace and balance. Thus, it can be seen as an opportunity for not just a relationship but a dynamic partnership, where the individuals are willing to change to support the union. With this energy, you can find not just a partner but your equal or your missing half.

In Chinese, when the character for man (*ren*) is added to the number TWO (*er*), it doesn't mean two men. It means a compassionate man showing the Yin quality of the number TWO. It also represents the Fire element (energy and creativity). Also, the number TWO suggests cooperation, a desire for understanding over all else.

TWO is thought a lucky number in Chinese culture based on the Chinese idiom "good things come in pairs." For example, when the Chinese character for happiness is written twice, it means "double happiness." This is often used in art and Feng Shui. It is used to bring about a great love relationship. In Cantonese, the

number TWO is made of the characters meaning "bright" and "easy."

TWO is represented by the Fire element. Fire is
about creativity and symbolizes when two come
together to create things.

IF YOU WANT MORE TWO ENERGY:

- have a comfortable porch swing for two or
  two chairs positioned for conversation.

- Have symmetrical pairs of plantings such
  as identical bushes flanking the walkway.

- Have a very cheery welcome mat, one
  that says "welcome" with symmetrical
  designs on it.

- For those living in an apartment, hang
  chimes in pairs on your balcony or patio
  on either side of the back door or sliders.

IF YOU WANT LESS TWO ENERGY:

- Have a bush of brightly colored flowers on
  only one side of the lawn or porch.

- Have a single chair on the porch.

- Paint your front door a bright color.

- Inside, hang most of the artwork on one
  side of the living room, leaving the other
  side empty and bare.

HOW TWO IS WRITTEN

The number TWO used to be written as two horizontal lines and is still written that way in Chinese. Our modern, Western TWO is really two horizontal lines but they are connected like two horizonal lines drawn without lifting the pen.

The most common ways to write the number TWO is either to have a flat base or to have a loop that ends with a tail. If your number TWO has a flat base, you are looking for stable relationships that won't change. If the base of your TWO is not flat but more rounded, you are seeking more balance and harmony in your relationships, understanding that sometimes there is a need for change and compromise. If there's a loop in the number TWO, there's a desire to hold on and encircle another person or pet. There's a strong inclination to protect the relationship and possibly exclude others who could be perceived as threats to the partnership.

It's so interesting that the number TWO looks like a FIVE upside down (or vice versa, since technically the TWO came first). So the energies of these two numbers are related. The excitement and adventure of the number FIVE is heightened when shared with another.

THE HOUSE NUMBER FONT OF TWO:

Notice the house number's font and style painted or attached to your home. A TWO with a flat base will help strengthen existing relationships and bring positive energy for a proper work/life balance for the people living in the home. If the font of the number TWO on the home has a loop, the relationships will be more intense and possibly to the extent of excluding others. There may be jealousy. Existing relationships will close ranks, protecting each other from outsiders, even extended family members. This is sometimes beneficial, but if the energy is too intense, it can be lessened through Feng Shui cures.

EXAMPLES OF TWO HOUSES

2: A dwelling with the house (or apartment) number TWO is ideal for bringing in a relationship or enhancing an existing relationship. There will be a desire to relate with your partner, do things together, and grow as a couple. The one difficulty with a TWO house is often similar to the number ONE house—it's on a corner. A corner house lacks symmetry, having only neighbors on one side that the TWO energy likes so much. This can produce the feeling that something essential is missing, causing the inhabitants to search for something continually. With a corner number TWO house, you can sometimes create balance through landscaping.

20: This is a potent fertility number, such that the couple meets the energy of the cosmic egg and thus can create a third (or fourth or fifth). It may be literal fertility, helping the couple bring a child into the world, or it can be the fruits of a project the couple works on together, like a book, music, or a creative business.

In the picture above, we see the house number spelled out. In this case, you would to consider the number of each letter and then add the numbers together. T=2, W=5, E=5, N=5, T=2, Y=7. 2+5+5+5+2+7=26. 2+6=8.

But when this person receives their mail or an official house listing is done then the number 20 would appear in the address. So it would be like a person named Robert but is friends call him Bob. In this case the formal name Robert is like the 20 in the house number. And the nickname, Bob, is how it's spelled out on the house itself. So the people living in the house may experience energy from both these numbers.

200: Here, the relationship energy gets extended, and the couple can stay together for a long time. However, honest communication is necessary to make time together truly happy. Those who live in the house may seek out friendships and business partnerships with others outside the home.

2000: With this house or apartment number, we see relationships going on and on no matter if it is beneficial or not. It's necessary to assess the relationship periodically and, though difficult, to release the relationship if it's not bringing happiness.

THREE

THE NUMBER OF CREATIVITY AND COMMUNICATION

The number THREE takes the power of the couple and brings forth a third. THREE facilitates connections, stimulates thinking, and brings creative ideas. This number's energy helps us reach outside of ourselves to draw in energy (i.e., people) to help and create with us. At the same time, it gives the freedom to express yourself authentically.

Historically the number THREE is associated with magic. Folk tales talk of genies offering three wishes or having three guesses to pass a test. Sometimes a magical person or creature came into being by saying their name three times. Some stories illustrate their morale through three different points of view using three characters. The Three Little Pigs, the Three Billy Goat's Gruff, and the Three Bears are all about living together and being a family and having different ways of doing things.

Overall, the energy of this number is social, expansive, and energetic. It also represents sexual creative power as well as the powers of observation and versatility. The energy of the number THREE is related to the triangle. In the three types of triangles, equilateral, isosceles, and scalene, the internal angles always add up to 180 degrees. It's as though three unique energies have come together, forming something whole and complete.

You might find living in this house gives you:

- A desire to work with others in the neighborhood, perhaps coordinating the neighborhood watch or the annual street yard sale.

- An interest in having more dinner parties, family game nights, or maybe hosting a book club.

- More friends in general and a desire to stay in touch.

- An inclination to develop a hobby or to focus on some creative aspect of your life.

Too Much THREE energy: Sometimes, the energy becomes out of balance, and there's too much THREE energy. This can happen because the home's outward appearance is so similar to the number's vibration, such as a THREE home with tympanum or gabled dormers over windows and doors or window oriels (a very tight three-sided bay window). Also, architectural details such as a very steep, pointed roofline or a hip roof or landscaping with bushes planted in groupings of three. It can also be because your name or birth number has a strong connection to the energy of THREE. For example, the name Clarence (the letters C and L both have the energy THREE.) Someone born on March 3 would already have so much THREE energy in their life that a THREE house could put them out of balance. The issue is that with so much THREE energy they carry personally, they will be naturally attracted to a THREE house. Too much THREE energy can make you irritable, easily angered, and very outspoken.

If the energy of this number is too strong, you may find yourself:

- Losing your temper very quickly, even to the point of throwing things or hitting things.

- Having accidents with fire when you cook/barbeque, burn candles, or light the fireplace.

- Saying things you don't mean to say (and saying them out loud.)

- Stockpiling creative or craft supplies but never finishing the projects.

CULTURAL MEANING

In the Christian tradition, THREE represents the Father, Son, and Holy Spirit. It is regarded as Body, Mind, and Spirit or Maid, Mother, and Crone in metaphysical circles. So in the West, the number THREE is seen as a complete number, representing creativity and communication.

In Asia, THREE is often used in popular sayings and proverbs to teach human virtues such as the saying, "after three days without reading, talk becomes flavorless," "a sly rabbit will have three openings to its den," and "three humble shoemakers brainstorming will make a great statesman."

In Chinese, THREE sounds like the Chinese word "alive" and the Chinese word. "birth," so it is deemed lucky. This also means there's increased fertility energy in a house with intense THREE energy. Not surprisingly, THREE is represented by the Wood element, a symbol of growth.

The number THREE is also thought to be lucky in Sweden and Italy.

IF YOU WANT MORE THREE ENERGY:

- Use a contrasting paint color to highlight gables over windows.

- Install awnings with a triangular hem.

- Cut bushes into a triangular shape or group bushes in threes.

- Inside, burn candles or put an electric candle in the window.

The house number is 723
The energy is THREE (7+2+3=12, 1+2=3).

The palladian windows
have pie-piece glass in
the arches like small
triangles

Multiple open gables
look like triangles and
increase the THREE
energy

Too much THREE energy can cause anger in the home and
people to be impatient. To shift this energy a single-tiered
fountain could be placed in the yard. Landscaping with
purple flowers would also help.

IF YOU WANT LESS THREE ENERGY:

- Draw the eyes away from a steep roofline
  and bring the energy downward by planting blue and purple flowers in the yard.

- Paint the house an earth-tone color, beige or brown.

- Add a water fountain to the front (but not a three-tiered one.)

- Inside keep the entryway very minimalist with no art or décor.

HOW THREE IS WRITTEN

In ancient writing, the number THREE was just three horizontal lines. It is still this way in Chinese. Our modern number THREE represents those three lines drawn without lifting the pen off the paper.

Visually the number THREE is like an EIGHT cut in half. The THREE can be drawn with a loop in the middle or not. The THREE has a rounded base, giving the impression it could rock back and forth. This means it is not stable but changeable. It's not closed off like an EIGHT, so it has an openness to new information. If your THREE has a flat base, then ideas become dogmatic even when new information is received.

If the upper half-circle is much smaller than the lower half-circle, your life's emphasis is practical application of ideas or making money over other concerns.

If your THREE is written with a loop in the center, you draw attention to the connection between your spiritual, intellectual side and your material, physical side. But it also can mean it takes more time for the spiritual part of you and the physical side of you to integrate and become one. This can manifest as having a career because it's practical rather than finding your true calling and doing something you love.

Sometimes the THREE is written with a flat top, sometimes called a "banker's three." This variant was said to be used to prevent criminally minded people from changing the THREE to an EIGHT. A flat-topped THREE suggests a level head and a practical mind not given to flights of fancy.

In Feng Shui, THREE is a Yang number and connected to the Wood element (growth and feeling alive.)

THE HOUSE NUMBER FONT OF THREE:

Notice the font and style of the house number painted on or attached to your home. A balanced THREE will bring happiness, interesting guests to visit, and lots of creative energy into the home. A THREE with a large lower half-circle will emphasize finances and getting stuff done. This could be beneficial in the short term, but the gains may feel shallow over time and not bring a profound satisfaction. If the THREE has a flat top, in addition to the other benefits the THREE energy brings, it will also give some protection from dishonesty in the home and threats from outside.

EXAMPLES OF THREE HOUSES

3: I spoke to a client, Karen, who just purchased a new home with house number THREE. Here's what I told her. *"Congratulations on your new home. You will like living in a THREE. A THREE house gives an energy of cooperation, creativity, and communication. That said, there can be bickering in a THREE house, especially if there are kids. I suggest you display or hang musical instruments in the living room or family room. You can use things like flutes or guitars (avoid things like drums). This will help there be harmonious communication between siblings. And for you, I suggest you plant roses by your front door to guard your heart in matters of love. In a THREE house, you must avoid any love triangles. Roses will attract love while the thorns will keep you safe from those who would be careless with your heart."*

30: Here, THREE comes together with the creative potential of ZERO to burst forth with creative energy. You will find opportunities for partnerships or cooperative ventures with people outside the home. There can be much success in business when you team up with others as well as happy personal relationships within the home.

300: With this number, the THREE energy attracts so many creative projects; it seems there is no way to finish them all. It is much easier to start another project than to bring the previous one to a close. You will need outside help to finish everything.

3000: With so many ZEROs, the brain sees so many possibilities, but nothing ever seems to get off the ground. Craft supplies sit in bags around the house. Catalogs of college classes lay amongst language software and unread books. It's more fun to dream about doing the creative endeavor and much more enjoyable to buy the supplies than actually work on the project.

FOUR

THE NUMBER OF HARD WORK, ENDINGS, AND LOSS

Chances are, if this number is on your door, it's the reason you picked up this book. This is the number that causes some potential house buyers and renters to flee. This number has had so much negative press studies show FOUR houses selling less than other comparable houses. This discount can make FOUR houses appealing to get into and hard to get out of.

The FOUR energy can be so solid and structured that it feels blocked or even stuck. It's methodical and practical, but having this energy around all the time can bring joyless days or give a repressive feeling. Strong FOUR energy can be very suspicious of others, so connections become limited.

But there's a silver lining here. There are ways to use the FOUR energy to your benefit, which we'll talk about in a moment. The number FOUR represents the four aspects of matter: animal, vegetable, mineral, and gaseous. There are four directions on the compass and four seasons in the year. The number FOUR represents stability, and having a strong, stable foundation. It represents being respectable, industrious, and tenacious. The energy of FOUR is organized and uses resources wisely.

You might find living in this house gives you:

- A solid work ethic, to the point of overwork.

- A desire to organize and economize, you hold on to things until they are used up or worn out.

- An inclination to start a business or move your business into your home.

- A desire to repair and maintain the house to a level where it takes up all your free time and extra resources.

FOUR represents the square or rectangle, a practical and solid shape. Sometimes the energy becomes out of balance, and there's too much FOUR energy. This can happen because the home's outward appearance is the same as the number's vibration, such as a FOUR home with a very boxy shape, a flat roof such as an adobe house, or an ultra-modern house. This can also be true if the house has a four-column portico or, in some cases, a very plain exterior. It can also be because your name or birth number has a strong connection to the energy of FOUR. For example, the first name David (the letters D and

V are both the energy FOUR), or someone born on April 4, would already have so much FOUR energy in their life that a FOUR house could put them out of balance. The challenge is with so much FOUR energy the person has personally, they will be naturally attracted to a FOUR house. If there's excessive FOUR energy, those living in the home can become depressed, suspicious, and dull. Things that held joy seem boring, and the people get trapped in a routine of endless work and house care.

If the energy of this number is too strong, you may find yourself:

- Working nights and weekends, taking a second job or even a third job.

- Finding it hard to throw things away or donate them, thinking you may need the item someday.

- Experiencing a series of losses such as losing a job, losing money in investments, struggling in relationships.

- Becoming fearful of things going on in the world, in your community, and the neighborhood.

CULTURAL MEANING

With the number FOUR, we find our first real split between Universal and cultural interpretations. In the West, we associate the number FOUR with the four elements; earth, air, fire, and water (as opposed to the Chinese five element system), the four suits of the playing cards, and the four legs of a table. It's about stability, practicality, and precision. Because of this, it is particularly beneficial in FOUR houses to have a home-based business. This energy is about hard work and valuing financial stability. FOUR encourages people to pay off debt, including the mortgage. For some, this energy feels very comfortable, and in that harmony, the family can prosper.

In Germany, the number FOUR is seen as a lucky number.

In many Asian countries, the number FOUR has the great misfortune to sound like the Chinese word for 'death,' so it is believed to be bad luck. This idea of the number FOUR being unlucky is spreading to many countries. We see more people become nervous about living in a FOUR. There's now a listed phobia of the number FOUR called tetraphobia.

This fear of the number FOUR has continued into other aspects of life. Many buildings in Asia have no fourth floor; in fact, some buildings in Hong Kong have skipped all floor numbers that have a FOUR in them, such as 14, 24, and 40-49. Some manufacturers in Asia don't use the number FOUR when naming projects such as cell phones, cars, or cameras. In Singapore, there are no public buses that have FOUR in the number. This is also true with phone numbers and hotel rooms—it's hard to find a number FOUR used.

The Chinese written character looks like the phrase 'clouds blocking the sun.' So again, we see no auspicious energy connected to FOUR. This gives us the impression there's no happiness to be had in a FOUR house.

Even the standard "404 error: Page not found" HTTP standard response code on the Internet seems to echo the negative energy of the number FOUR.

Even though FOUR is in Chinese associated with the word "death," living in a FOUR house would not necessarily mean you would die in that house, but instead, there would be lessons about letting go and endings. People in the home would examine relationships and friendships and end those that aren't bringing benefit. Since the FOUR energy is both about endings and holding on, often people struggle with decluttering. They want to get the most use out of things while trying to release what is no longer truly needed.

Living in a FOUR house can also affect your ability to sell the house later. A study done in British Columbia found that homes with strong FOUR energy (numbers like 4, 14, 44, etc.) sold for 2.2 percent less than the average home. That may not sound like much, but in an expensive area, that could mean a $20,000 price difference or more.

If you find yourself living in a FOUR, you'll want to channel the less positive energy away from you and your family while retaining the benefits of the FOUR. As previously mentioned having a business in your home is one way to do this. The energy of the FOUR is to work hard and learn to let go of things (let things die that need to die). It's necessary not to let clutter accumulate. If you consistently let excess stuff go, you could find this home very beneficial for you.

FOUR is a Yin number and of the Metal element (productivity, organization, and material wealth).

The energy of FOUR can affect the home even if there's a FOUR in the number. If you choose the apartment number 428, the FOUR energy is softened by the other numbers, but the energy still exists. The energy of 428 reads, 'by letting go, we find balance and harmony, which leads to happiness.' Now, these three numbers are all yin so that changes would happen more slowly, almost imperceptibly, but they would still happen.

IF YOU WANT MORE FOUR ENERGY:

- Have a front door with molding that forms squares or a pattern of squares.

- Paint trim around windows a contrasting color or install lintels painted in a contrasting color.

- Cut bushes into squares and rectangulars.

- Have furniture inside with sharp angles and clean lines.

Number FOUR energy is strong, rigid and unyielding.

106363898 © creativecommonsstockphotos – Dreamstime.com

Traditional brick or stone can give a house a very solid appearance but if the house is also a number FOUR it can make the residents feel blocked, repressed or sad.

82963918 © creativecommonsstockphotos – Dreamstime.com

This house number is 49
The energy is FOUR (4+9=13, 1+3=4).

The gambrel style roof can also emphasize FOUR energy. Though in this house only the front gable has the typical gambrel four-sided roof. The flat roof at the top of the house is FOUR energy

The FOUR energy is is very strong due to the pronounced colums as you face the house.

Too much FOUR energy can cause people to work too hard and have losses.The roof line and columns are permanent fixtures and can't be easily changed. Anything that can soften the front appearance of the house would help such as adding foliage and painting the house a darker color.

IF YOU WANT LESS FOUR ENERGY:

- Add rounded shapes such as bushes and trees cut in organic, rounded shapes.

- Have a curved walkway to the front door.

- Put rings of stone under trees and add flowers.

- Have round furniture inside, round pillows, and an overstuffed sofa.

HOW FOUR IS WRITTEN

There are two ways to write the number FOUR, one with the closed top and the other with the top open. In ancient times, in the Middle East, the number FOUR was written as a cross. Over time the top bar was connected to the middle in a single stroke to form the closed top FOUR we know today.

Some are surprised this number is associated with stability since it stands on only one leg instead of having a solid base. But its history as a cross (covering all angles) is what makes it so solid. Take note that though this energy is about practicality and hard work, most of the work done is on the spiritual and intellectual planes because most of the written number is in the upper part of the figure.

A closed-top implies a mind that already has a plan and is ready to implement it. The open-top suggests an openness and that plans are fluid. The person is open to change. Too much of the number FOUR will bring a lot of tedious work, a weak suspicious mind, and extreme stubbornness.

THE HOUSE NUMBER FONT OF FOUR:

In fonts and typefaces, the leg of the number FOUR often falls below the baseline. It's like it's drilling into the earth like a flagpole planted and strong. This increases the stable energy and decreases flexibility.

EXAMPLES OF FOUR HOUSES

4: Not all FOUR homes are unlucky, but they are almost always associated with hard work. #4 E 80th Street in Manhattan is home to one of the most expensive real estate in the United States. It was owned by a descendant of the Woolworth family who's retail chain dominated most of the 20th century. This home was completed in 1916, including an entryway so massive it has three closets. The dining room can seat 50 guests, and the front drawing-room is 35 feet long. This home is worth more than 21 million dollars. Besides hard work, this number brings thrift. The Woolworth stores were noted for their lower prices and good value.

40: This number emphasizes the need to release and let go of excess. Having a business in the home is the best way to use this energy. A 40 house or apartment would do well with businesses selling a product (the ZERO would represent inventory turnover) or performing a service that helps people release something, such as professional organizing (releasing excess stuff), counseling (releasing emotional issues), healthcare (releasing illness) or weight loss.

400: Here, the energy of the number FOUR becomes more intense. Work and effort seem to increase as the years go by. The house may need more repairs, and the yard may need constant care. Clutter can take over the house. There may be a desire to horde supplies in case of some future disaster. Stuff is kept just because it may have some potential use. As clutter accumulates, money flow can slow to a trickle. It's essential in this house to live with a minimum of things. Choose what you love and use and discard the rest. Don't hold on, or else you may stop the flow of abundance.

4000: With three ZEROS, the energy of the FOUR affects the family. Family and friends come to the house and stay. A week's visit turns into months. The home could pass down to children or grandchildren. The house can fill with the belongings of relatives. And while the house gains in value, the profits are eaten away by repairs and maintenance.

FIVE

THE NUMBER OF CHANCE AND CHANGE

FIVE sits in the middle of the numbers and acts as a balance point, similar to a fulcrum and a lever. So with FIVE, a small action can yield a significant result. We also see FIVE as an ice skater spinning on a single skate. All is in motion and can stop at any point finding a new direction. FIVE is about adventure and opportunity but also chance and change.

In geometry, FIVE forms the pentagon and the five points of the star (the pentacle). These are geometric figures that are considered lucky and strong. The number FIVE represents a balance at the center. In a house, the number FIVE might be represented by a five-sided window though this is rare. FIVE can make life exciting, bringing opportunities for success and help you break free of old patterns.

FIVE houses are often homes under renovation or restoration. The energy can be so constant that construction or decorating is never really finished. The house expands by adding rooms or by creating an outdoor room in the backyard. Inside, artwork and design elements can be prominent. FIVE houses also tend to have craft rooms, sewing rooms, or workshops.

You might find living in this house gives you:

- A sense of adventure about life and a desire to take risks.

- A love of parties and an inclination to do more entertaining at home.

- A desire to renovate the house primarily to make it stand out in the neighborhood.

- A desire to flip the house and move on to the next project.

Sometimes the energy becomes out of balance, and there's too much FIVE energy. This can happen because the outward appearance of the home mirrors the vibration of the number FIVE. A home with Dutch gables (gables with a rounded top) or a mansard roofline would be examples. Houses in need of fixing-up or with very uneven landscaping, fallen trees, or overgrown foliage are also examples. Houses that have pentagon-shaped windows or are architecturally unique have intense FIVE energy. Or it can be because your name or birth number also has a connection to the energy of FIVE. For example, the first name Edward has the letter E and the letter W are both the energy FIVE. Someone born on May 5 would already have so much FIVE energy in their life that a FIVE house could put them out of balance. The difficulty is, with so much FIVE energy they carry personally, they will be naturally attracted to a FIVE house. People not used to a lot of change can find the energy of FIVE difficult. There can be changes in jobs, relationships, and shifts in the stability of the family.

If the energy of this number is too strong, you may find yourself:

- Wanting to play all the time, being hooked on video games or online games.

- Taking unreasonable or unnecessary risks with money.

- Taking up extreme sports or other risky behavior.

- Continually renovating the house, starting the next project before the first one is finished.

CULTURAL MEANING

FIVE, like FOUR, is seen differently in different cultures. In some cultures, the number FIVE is lucky. It represents the balance of the five elements in Chinese philosophy: Wood, Fire, Earth, Metal, and Water. When all five of these elements are present, they form a creative cycle, each creating the next in the circle, thus bringing continual success and opportunity.

FIVE is a Yang number and is used to count many elements in Chinese thought. In addition to the five elements, there are five senses, five emotions (anger, grief, worry, fear, and joy), five vital organs (heart, liver, stomach, lungs, and kidneys), and the five directions (North, South, East, West, and Center) just to name a few.

There is one issue with FIVE. It does sound like the Chinese word for 'nothing,' but this can have a benefit. When it's paired with an unlucky number, it can negate the bad luck. For example, the number 54 means "no death." But if paired with a fortunate number, the FIVE can cancel out the good energy. For example, the number

Number FIVE energy is colorful, social and fun.

108523844 © Publicdomainphotos – Dreamstime.com

Colorful houses really stand out and make a statement but if the house is also a number FIVE it can make the residents feel reckless and crave extreme experiences.

193764 © Jose Fuente – Dreamstime.com

58 means "not prosperous." For the most part, FIVE is deemed a positive number, balanced

and complete bringing many opportunities for adventure and fun.

IF YOU WANT MORE FIVE ENERGY:

- Paint the house a bright color or many colors.

- Have visible signs of renovation projects in process (piles of garden bricks ready to lay, lumber, plants in temporary pots.)

- Have a workshop in the home or a workshop in the garage.

- Inside the house, have bright colored or unique artwork.

IF YOU WANT LESS FIVE ENERGY:

- Keep exterior colors, including plants, very neutral.

- Have more symmetry in landscaping, avoid over planting on one side instead keep the different areas of the yard balanced.

- Avoid displaying holiday flags and decorations, remove weathervanes.

- Inside, keep décor to a minimum and choose sedate, muted colors.

HOW FIVE IS WRITTEN

There are several ways to draw the number FIVE. Look at how you have written yours. Is the top attached? Is the top written in a separate stroke from the rest of the number? Is the lower loop large or small? The FIVE is like the TWO reversed in form, so now the stability (the straight stroke) is in the mental and spiritual area, and the curved bottom allows it to rock back and forth in the physical world, allowing for much change. Writing the FIVE in one motion can indicate that in moments of change, the mental work comes first. This might sound good, but we can't always predict the extent of change, so we may end up unprepared and have to improvise. When the top stroke is written last, the physical changes occur first, and then the mental and spiritual interpretation and integration follows. If the top stroke is not attached, it can indicate the mental process is not connected to the change happening in life. It's like the mind is 'flying away' from the experience of the body.

THE HOUSE NUMBER FONT OF FIVE:

In many fonts and typefaces, the bottom of the FIVE extends below the line. This is called a descender. It means that the number FIVE reaches below the surface into our basest desires and brings our secrets and hidden wishes to the surface.

EXAMPLES OF FIVE HOUSES

5: This house number brings the energy of being at a crossroads. In this home, you will be faced with decisions about career, relationship, and family life that, once made, will not let you go back. While that sounds dire, there are great benefits in going forward. There will be much change in this home. An excellent solution is to move the furniture around periodically or change room colors to shift the energy from yourself back to the home itself.

50: Here, we combine the energy of FIVE (the star) with the circle forming the energy of a pentagram, a power symbol in times past. Like DaVinci's Vitruvian Man, the energy is about keeping everything in proportion. There will be a strong need to balance your work and family life in this home. You will feel a desire to renovate to make the home more comfortable. Redecorating efforts will often be focused on leisure or party areas of the house.

In the picture above, the number five is much larger and is lower than the zero. T`his emphasizes the physical or material characteristics of the number. The number five can be very sociable so this would indicate that there could be a lot of parties and fun in the house. And then when you add in the zero, the party goes on and on.

500: Here, the energy of change becomes more intense. You find yourself wanting to do major renovations on the home or creative projects pile up around the house. If the energy is channeled to yourself and your family, you may find yourselves making big decisions about career, travel, or education that take the family in a whole new direction. This is an excellent house to have parties in, but you may find the party never stops, and the guests stay long after you thought they would leave.

5000: With this number, the energy of change and risk-taking intensifies. You may find yourself drawn to extreme sports and wild travel adventures. You may decorate the house very eclectically, using unusual materials or building techniques. If the energy is not expressed in the home's architecture, you may find that your life is continually changing. This number would lend itself well to someone who works as an independent contractor or has a very unusual profession.

SIX

THE NUMBER OF AFFECTION AND DOMESTIC HARMONY

SIX is about comfort, caring, and loving peace. It is a nurturing number and focuses energy on taking care of others. It represents prosperity in a general sense, like having food in the house and a working car in the garage. We also associate SIX with artistic ability, music and poetry, imagination, and intelligence.

Even though a cube gives us the impression of the number FOUR, a cube actually has six sides. Here we see the connection between these two numbers. While SIX doesn't have the restrictions and blocks that FOUR does, it does like the order and neatness both in the home and in life. That doesn't always mean the house will be super clean, instead certain areas of the house will be highly organized and efficient.

SIX houses have a warmth to them. This could be due to the color of the house, or a prominent chimney, or through window boxes with flowers and a very welcoming front porch. The landscaping tends to be a bit overgrown but otherwise well maintained. Everywhere you look seems brimming with life.

You might find living in this house gives you:

- A desire to have children or to fill your house with extended family.

- A home where the neighborhood children come to play.

- An inclination to cook at home and do other domestic projects.

- To have pets and/or to welcome birds with bird feeders or bring butterflies with flowering bushes.

Sometimes the energy becomes out of balance, and there's too much SIX energy. This can

happen because the home's outward appearance is already like the number, such as a SIX
home with intricate cutouts on the balustrades
as in a Swiss cottage, "storybook" architecture
like that seen in old Victorian houses, or landscaping like a small botanical garden. Or it can
be because your name or birth number also has
a strong connection to the energy of SIX. For
example, the first name Flora (the letters F and
O are both the energy SIX.) Someone born on
June 6 would already have so much SIX energy
in their life that a SIX house could put them out
of balance. The interesting fact is that with so
much SIX energy that they carry personally,
they will be naturally attracted to a SIX house.

Excessive SIX energy can cause you not to want
to leave the house, even when it's beneficial to
do so. You may find yourselves staying home and
shunning the world. And too much SIX energy
can make a person feel complacent, obsessed
with feelings, or conversely too focused on triv-
ial household things.

If the energy of this number is too strong, you
may find yourself:

   · Becoming obsessed with having more
     children or more pets.

   · Finding yourself afraid to go out into the
     world, procrastinating whenever it's time
     to leave the house.

- Being short of money because you keep giving it to relatives and friends in need.

- Hoarding food, buying more groceries even when you already have a full pantry.

CULTURAL MEANING

The number SIX means prosperity in Asia. SIX is a Yin number and is deemed lucky because it sounds like the Chinese word for 'good luck.' Combining a SIX with an odd number makes it even luckier because there is a balance of Yin and Yang.

It's associated with the Water element of communication and flow. It is also associated with discernment; there's an old saying in Chinese that a person should see the six colors of black: dark black, light black, dry black, wet black, deep black, and white-black (gray).

In Mandarin, the number SIX sounds like the Chinese word for "flowing." When several sixes are strung together, the energy is about smooth, frictionless flow and is regarded as very favorable for business. In Asia, high amounts of money have been paid for phone numbers or license plates with many sixes.

In Kabbalistic Judaism, three sixes, 666, is the number that represents perfection in this world.

In the West, the number six is not looked at as lucky and is especially unlucky if it's written three times. In Christianity, the number 666 is so unlucky that there is currently no 666 area code in the United States. This is a reference from the Bible Book of Revelations chapter 13 verse 17–18, "and he provides that no one will be able to buy or to sell, except the one who has the mark, either the name of the beast or the number of his name. Here's the wisdom. Let him who has understanding calculate the number of the beast, for the number is that of a man; and his number is six hundred and sixty-six." There are plenty of house numbers that are 666. If you buy a house with house number 666, know that later, depending on the area of the world you live in, you may have issues selling it.

IF YOU WANT MORE SIX ENERGY:

- Add plantings to the garden with whimsical touches such as gazing balls, gnomes, and garden fairies, or add edible plantings and fruit trees.

- Install children's play equipment, a treehouse, or a playhouse.

- Add gingerbread trim (fancifully cut frieze boards) around doors and roof overhangs or column brackets.

- Inside, have a cook's kitchen with displayed pots and pans and a well-stocked spice-rack.

IF YOU WANT LESS SIX ENERGY:

- Cut landscaping into very regular shapes or consider xeriscaping with rocks and native plants only.

- Have a straight and narrow walkway with plants cut back, away from the walkway.

- Post a "no trespassing" or "no soliciting" sign.

- Inside, avoid displaying any family photos in the entryway or living room.

HOW SIX IS WRITTEN

In ancient times the number SIX was written as a downward stroke with a loop in the center. Over time the loop became more pronounced, and the line ended with the loop.

When the SIX is written, most of the figure is in the lower loop, representing the physical and material realms. This gives it the energy of nurturing like an affectionate parent rocking a child to sleep. The SIX responds to physical changes by not over-thinking or over-planning but using creativity to find solutions. If your SIX is written with the loop closed, it is the energy of completing the circuit, and everything gets taken care of. The open SIX loop, while open to more experiences, can feel more detached in relationships.

THE HOUSE NUMBER FONT OF SIX:

Sometimes, the number SIX is written with a line underneath to distinguish it from the number NINE. This grounds the energy and makes it even more practical and connected to the physical experience.

EXAMPLES OF SIX HOUSES

6: A SIX home can be warm and inviting. Find a space for a dining room table and gather the family there for evening meals. If you want to get pregnant, a SIX home can be ideal, as it's easy to attract fertility energy there. SIX homes also work well if you have a career in medicine, customer service, or childcare.

60: Possibly the best number for getting pregnant, this combines the energy of SIX with the ZERO, representing the egg of potentiality. This also works well if you're in a creative profession, writing a book, doing graphic design, making videos. You can prosper in this house.

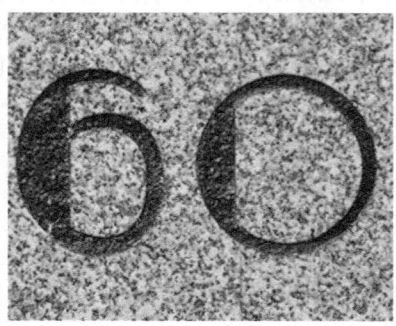

In the picture above, the number 60 is written in a kind of Art Deco style. The emphasis is at the beginning of each of the digits. This would indicate that there is more energy for beginnings than there is for endings or for the process in the middle. The people living in the house need to make sure to finish what they start instead of just starting new things over and over.

600: The two ZEROs intensify the energy. The home is still very fertile, but now children may not want to leave home. Relatives may come and stay for extended periods. And you may find yourself taking in stray animals or adopting many pets. This home works well if you are in a **humanitarian profession such as running a nonprofit.**

6000: Now the energy is out of balance; with so much caring for others, there is little time to take care of self. This can lead to health problems where one is forced to pay attention to their own body and their own needs. It's essential in this house to schedule time for self-care. Learn to ask for help before you need to ask for help.

SEVEN

THE NUMBER OF INTELLECT AND BELIEF

Universally this number is connected to the mysteries of the world. The seven days of the week were named after the five visible planets and the two luminaries: Sun, moon, Mercury, Venus, Mars, Jupiter, and Saturn. The number SEVEN is connected to the cycle of the week and, therefore, the rhythm of life. There are seven colors of the rainbow: red, orange, yellow, green, blue, indigo, and violet. There are seven notes on the musical scale.

Houses that have intense SEVEN energy often display spiritual or religious icons both inside and out. There will be a strong desire for education and learning. Therefore, a private library or reading nook is often found in the house. People in the house will want to display certificates, diplomas, or other awards where they were recognized for their knowledge and achievements. This number represents spirituality, magical powers, dreams, fantasy, beliefs, and a love of ideas.

SEVEN is the result of 3+4, "thought plus structure." Here we see thinking put to concrete use. A SEVEN sided figure is called a heptagon, a shape you hardly ever see in architecture.

You might find living in this house gives you:

- A desire to study, attend University, or to teach.

- Opportunities to become more spiritual or religious, to attend services and connect with others of your faith.

- A desire to get active politically, work the polls, or volunteer to help someone campaign or even run for office yourself.

- To play an instrument, form a band, or play music all the time.

Sometimes the energy becomes out of balance, and there's too much SEVEN energy. This happens because the home's outward appearance mirrors the number's vibration, such as a SEVEN home with sparse, neglected landscaping or a house that looks out of place on the lot either by the way it faces or because of the surrounding buildings. It can also be because of a perpetually full mailbox or a porch littered with circulars. Or it can be because your name or birth number also have a strong connection to the energy of SEVEN. For example, the first name Paige (the letters P and G are both the energy SEVEN.) Someone born on July 7 would already have so much SEVEN energy in their life that a SEVEN house could put them out of balance. The real challenge is, with so much SEVEN energy they carry personally, they will be naturally attracted to a SEVEN house.

If there's too much of the energy of SEVEN, the person living in the house can become a recluse, the family may be unsocial with neighbors, or the people living in the house can be misunderstood in their community. Too much of the energy of SEVEN can bring arguments in the home. There can be differences in opinions in politics and religion. There can be a desire to be right rather than to be happy.

When there's too much SEVEN energy, it can lead to moodiness, confusion, and a contempt for the practical aspects of living. People can become overly passionate about their beliefs, with such a desire to express themselves that they can't hear other people's ideas. This can lead to isolation. Too much SEVEN energy can lead to such certainty one is right that the person becomes aloof and sarcastic towards others. This can lead to breakups in relationships and separations in the family.

If the energy of this number is too strong, you may find yourself:

- At odds with neighbors over politics like political signs in their yards or yours.

- Arguing at home or with neighbors over religion or worldly affairs.

- Feeling or being under surveillance or noticing a neighbor under surveillance by police or other authorities.

- Feeling isolated, wanting to sell the home and leave the area or even the country.

CULTURAL MEANING

It's often easy to find rental houses that are the number SEVEN. SEVEN houses can have more turnover of tenants than other houses as people struggle with following the rules set by a landlord or because they struggle to make ends meet financially. They may be more focused on education or saddled with student loan debt.

We, here in the West, often connect SEVEN with its rhyming word "heaven." SEVEN is associated with spiritual thought but also often used in gambling and other games of chance. Oddly though, breaking a mirror is said to give you seven years bad luck.

SEVEN is a Yang number and used warily in the East as it is associated with rituals of death, including the *qiqi* ritual where the soul of the dead passes through the gates of hell. Other numbers mitigate this energy. So if you live in number 179, the numbers 1 and 9 help ease the disharmony of the 7. The components of the number show us the energy in the house. The 1 represents unity, the 7, death and through that loss, gaining a greater understanding, and the 9 longevity. Putting this all together, it could read, 'by uniting your mind, body, and spirit, you wisely let go of things not serving you, thus increasing your longevity.' And since all the numbers are odd or Yang numbers, you will do this with a great deal of energy. You may find yourself completely revamping your diet, letting go of old hurts that block your forward progress, or aggressively removing clutter from your home and with it removing perhaps toxic or other harmful substances that stand in the way of your long life.

The number SEVEN is neutral in Feng Shui, bringing no harm but not attracting prosperity as some other numbers can. In Feng Shui, SEVEN is the Fire element (creativity and energy). There is a festival in China on the seventh day of the seventh month (sometimes called the "ghost month") and a story that tells of the seventh daughter of the king of heaven. On this one day, she is allowed to be with her lover, and the rest of the time, she is separated from him, so she is despondent.

The number SEVEN is thought lucky for relationships in the Far East because it sounds like the word "togetherness." This is in contrast to the Western meaning of SEVEN being the lone voice in the wilderness or a single flag blowing in the breeze. In Chinese, it also sounds like the word "two arise," so some do consider this number lucky, but most often, this number has both positive and negative qualities and is very much subject to the surrounding numbers to see how it manifests.

IF YOU WANT MORE SEVEN ENERGY:

- Create tree rings with bricks standing on their ends (like books lined up on a shelf but in a circle around a tree.)

- Hang religious or spiritual symbols on your porch.

- Display a flag of your country or your favorite sports team.

- In an apartment just inside the door, have a symbol of your most cherished belief (religious, political, or ideological.)

IF YOU WANT LESS SEVEN ENERGY:

- Soften the exterior by adding rounded shapes in the form of flowers and bushes.

- Decorate your yard or porch in a similar way to the neighbors.

- Remove gates or bars from the porch or walkway

- \sayings, and only have a minimum number of books or no books displayed at all.

HOW SEVEN IS WRITTEN

How the number SEVEN is written has not changed much over the years, though it used to have a more curved top, and the vertical line would come down straight. Now we see it with a flat top, and the vertical line is drawn at an angle.

In modern times the number SEVEN is drawn several ways. The simplest is the short-stroke on top, continuing downward at an angle to the base. Sometimes we see a small hook at the beginning of the short stroke. There is also the SEVEN drawn with the horizontal cross stroke in the center. The drawn SEVEN is related to the ONE except for the top, which seems to be "caught in the wind," indicating that thoughts and ideas rule. It is because SEVEN stands on just one leg, usually at an angle; the focus is less on the practical and more on the ideal. When the hook at the top is added, we see a desire to grab and hold on to ideas. When the horizontal stroke cuts the SEVEN in half, we see a division between heaven and earth, between the mind and the body. Perhaps this is an attempt to stabilize the thoughts and vision, or it can be a total separation of what a person thinks and what they do.

THE HOUSE NUMBER FONT OF SEVEN.

Now notice the font and style of the house number painted on or attached to your home. If the SEVEN is lower than the other numbers, it seems "dug in," more focused on making a stand for ideals. If the SEVEN sits higher than the other numbers, it can mean one wants to be "above it all" or keep to the moral high ground. In a positive light, this can mean sticking to principles, but it can also isolate oneself because you may regard others as less savvy or less educated.

EXAMPLES OF SEVEN HOUSES

7: SEVEN houses can be filled with the energy of education and intellectual pursuits. They can be houses of faith, allowing religion to guide in daily practices. With so much thought in spiritual and mental realms, the practical can be forgotten. Living in a SEVEN house requires the family to pay attention to things like jobs, bills, and getting meals ready. The inclination is to let these things slide because learning, praying, or meditating seem more vital.

70: Now we combine the energy of the number SEVEN with the creative potential of ZERO, and here there's energy that can produce great writers, musicians, preachers, and teachers. The thoughts and ideas get spread into the world, even if it's just locally or on a blog. Here intellect and ideas are looking for an audience.

700: With this number, the energy increases but becomes more challenging to fulfill. The desire to write or put ideas out into the world is compelling, but the need for perfection gets in the way of getting the concepts on paper. The people living in the house become frustrated, even screaming their ideas and opinions at anyone who will listen but finding no true outlet. Everyone is talking over everyone else, and no one is listening.

7000: This energy can manifest in several ways. Books and papers can take over the house. There may be hoarding of newspapers and magazines, stacks piled to the ceiling. There can be an overwhelming amount of information through technology. The TV is always on and the family members are individually focused on their devices or computers without ever hearing one another. While this may be a single person in a house all alone, stuck in their thoughts, feeling isolated and angry with the world.

EIGHT

THE NUMBER OF SUCCESS AND MANIFESTATION

EIGHT is the number of material success and a popular number in many cultures. It represents cycles and time. When set on its side is the symbol for infinity. It shows the potential for reversals in all aspects of our lives. Being poor one day doesn't mean you will be poor forever, but being rich doesn't ensure that you will always be rich. The EIGHT is hardworking and has both tenacity and follow-through. While EIGHT is not necessarily about risk-taking, it is about putting your heart and soul into a project and seeing what success you can make. EIGHT.

EIGHT is the most visually balanced of the numbers, and it represents success, power, wisdom, and wealth. In architecture, we see the number EIGHT in the eight sides of an octagon, an influential shape in Feng Shui. It is based on the eight trigrams of the I Ching found in the center ring of the Feng Shui compass, the Lo Pan. It's considered fortunate to have an octagon-shaped window in a home.

EIGHT is related to the eight phases of the moon: new, crescent, first quarter, gibbous, full, disseminating, last quarter, and balsamic, which shows the cycle of regeneration and degeneration, that things grow and then diminish, but then they grow again.

You might find living in this house gives you:

- Money opportunities you have not experienced before.

- A desire, energy, and excitement to get ahead in your career or to expand your business.

- An interest in using meditation, visualization, and prayer for manifesting material desires.

- An inclination to work hard, but balancing that with relaxing vacations and well-deserved time off.

Sometimes the energy becomes out of balance, and there's too much EIGHT energy. This can happen because the home's outward appearance is so similar to the vibration of the number, such as an EIGHT home with many octagon windows, gaudy architectural features such as turrets, Grecian columns, or castle-like features. We can also feel this energy if the house is much larger than the surrounding homes, such as a two-story mansion among one-story cottages. Or it can be because your name or birth number also has a strong connection to the energy of EIGHT. For example, the first name Zach (the letters Z and H are both the energy of EIGHT.) Someone born on August 8 would already have so much EIGHT energy in their life that an EIGHT house could put them out of balance. The trouble is with so much EIGHT energy they carry personally, they will be naturally attracted to an EIGHT house.

If there is too much of the EIGHT energy, the inhabitants will think of nothing but business. Their lives are consumed with the ideas of profit and sales. The home can bring out unscrupulous instincts in people who feel they need these tactics to get ahead in a challenging world. Too much EIGHT energy can cause the homeowners or residents to be ruthless and stubborn.

If the energy of this number is too strong, you may find yourself:

- Fighting with friends and family over financial or business dealings.

- Being the victim of fraud or theft.

- In lawsuits with neighbors or former business connections.

- Thinking of everything in life in terms of business and profit.

CULTURAL MEANING

To us in the West, the EIGHT shape shows that what we can dream in our heart, we can manifest in our world. The number EIGHT is the only number where the top half is the same as the bottom half, so, it calls to mind the famous inscription on the Emerald Tablet, "as above so below." This number represents money and power and manifesting your ideas (above) in your world (below). With EIGHT, we see the potential to manifest heaven on earth.

EIGHT is a Yin number connected to the Chinese words for 'wealth' and 'to prosper.' It is also a significant number representing the eight trigrams of the I Ching and the eight immortals—those who have achieved "immortality" (being remembered throughout the ages) through pious living and meditation. The prized lotus flower has eight petals. In Feng Shui, it is the Wood element (growth and expansion).

Famously, the 2008 Olympics, held in China, officially began on 8-8-08, at 8:08:08 PM local time. In fact, there is such a demand for the number EIGHT there are reports of large sums being paid for phone numbers and license plates containing the number EIGHT, including a phone number with all EIGHTS, which sold for the equivalent of $260,000.

The EIGHT is considered so lucky that '88' is called "double happiness," the ideal number for a happy marriage. EIGHT resembles the Chinese character of 'happiness,' and so two EIGHTS would be 'double happiness.' This character is seen at weddings and birthdays and also in decorations, jewelry, and pottery.

IF YOU WANT MORE EIGHT ENERGY:

- Add some external architectural feature that shows your house's value, such as a solid wood garage door or stone driveway.

- Have the yard professionally cared for and manicured.

- Hang large stained-glass octagon art pieces in windows.

- Inside, create a grand entryway using high-end materials such as marble, fine wood, and brass.

IF YOU WANT LESS EIGHT ENERGY:

- Add chairs or a bench to the front porch.

- Add small whimsical art pieces to the yard, such as bunnies, angels, and shiny objects.

- Remove gates or leave gates open.

Variations on the Number EIGHT

When the number EIGHT is drawn as two concentric circles there can be a separation between what you want to have happen and what does happen.

When the lower loop is larger on the number EIGHT there is more emphasis on results. There may be less planning and more doing.

Occasionally you can find the number EIGHT drawn with a larger upper loop. This energy supports planning and thinking things through before taking action. .

- Inside, display family portraits and vacation pictures in the entryway of the home.

HOW EIGHT IS WRITTEN

In the beginning, the number EIGHT was drawn more like a FIVE in a kind of 'S' shape. Later, so the two numbers were not confused, people began connecting the end stroke with the beginning, forming the EIGHT we see today.

EIGHT can be drawn in a continuous pattern, or it can be done as two circles. Just the act of drawing the continuous line is like drawing power down from heaven to help you with what you need on earth. If the EIGHT is made with two circles, you separate heaven from earth, separating your vision from what could be your reality. If the two circles don't touch, then there is no connection of thoughts and spirit to what is trying to be accomplished in the world. This can bring many challenges, especially wanting to be right over being happy.

The EIGHT drawn in the continuous pattern can also have a larger loop either on the top or the bottom. A larger loop on top emphasizes the mind and spirit, while a larger lower loop emphasizes the material and physical. We talked earlier about how the number THREE is half of the number EIGHT. Here we see how the EIGHT can take our ideas and bring us the help we need to complete what we have set out to do. EIGHT is a powerful number, and an excess of EIGHT brings more severe consequences such as materialism, massive failure, ruthlessness, and jealousy.

THE HOUSE NUMBER FONT OF EIGHT:

Often, house numbers favor a larger lower loop. This brings a focus to the material or practical aspects of home care. This can be emphasized if the number sits lower than other numbers.

EXAMPLES OF EIGHT HOUSES

8–This house is lucky. It's ideal for people with big ideas and who want to make their mark in the world. This house number also helps the family find a balance between the physical world and their spiritual lives. It's best to have a home business or to own a business to get the most out of this positive energy. At the very least, a small office at home to reap the benefits.

80–This number adds a third circle to the mix. Now we have so much potential; opportunities are everywhere. People living in this home will think big and find it easy to take their thoughts and ideas and turn them into actions in the real world. However, it is possible to have so many irons in the fire you don't know what to focus on. Try to stay grounded and be practical. This will bring the most success.

800–Now the potential becomes so intense it carries you and your family with it. It's easy to be caught up in the momentum or circumstances that arise. One small step sets you on a path, such as accepting a job or investing in a company. You find yourself committed to a much bigger endeavor than you first realized.

This is a good number for the people who want to shape the future or shake up the world.

8000–The energy becomes overwhelming. The all-consuming thought is about growing income or expanding the business, or increasing the family's power. The people in the house either feel there is plenty of time, so they end up squandering it or feel there's no time and work day and night to achieve their goals.

NINE

THE NUMBER OF LONGEVITY AND LUCK

NINE is a positive number with a somewhat complex meaning. Its energy takes care of oneself and takes care of the world, being both introspective and outward thinking. This energy looks for prosperity, and yet it's humanitarian. In taking care of yourself and caring for others, you focus on the spiritual meaning and bigger picture of life. Under the energy of this number, you gather what you want but only hold on to what you need and release all else. NINE is about collecting all the information, discerning what is of value, and then letting go of what does not or will not serve you.

NINE represents the nine directions (north, northeast, east, southeast, south, southwest, west, and northwest) and the center. This is the wisdom that comes from considering options in all directions or options.

This number is sometimes seen as a sign of wishes coming true. The NINE energy means you've done all the prep work ahead of time, and then the opportunity appears. You have the wisdom and courage to take the path to what you've been wanting.

The number NINE is about longevity. It signals the end of a cycle, a time to get ready for something new. NINE is about continually ending old cycles and beginning new cycles. Through this flow of energy, true longevity can be achieved.

You might find living in this house gives you:

- A sense of peace, not perhaps every day but more often than you have experienced in other houses.

- A desire to whittle possessions down to only what you need,

- An interest in keeping yourself healthy through diet and exercise.

- Lots of unexpected luck and synchronicity.

Sometimes the energy gets out of balance, and there's too much NINE energy. This can happen because the home's outward appearance mirrors the number's vibration, such as a NINE home decorated with Syrian arches or with many architectural features such as in Victorian houses. It shows up in very old houses, especially historic buildings, or if there are old trees around the dwelling. Or it can be because your name or birth number has a strong connection to the NINE energy. A person named Irene (the letters I and R both have the energy of NINE.) Someone born on September 9 would already have so much NINE energy in their life that a NINE house could put them out of balance. The challenge is that with so much NINE energy that they carry personally, they will be naturally drawn to a NINE house.

When there is too much NINE energy, the inhabitants can become impatient with others who may not be as far along in their careers or on the path they've chosen. Simultaneously, they may be sensitive to any criticism received from either people living with them or neighbors. This can bring on quarrels in the home. They also may become the victim of deception or fraud because of their desire to live in peace, no matter the cost. NINE energy can lead to minimalism, but only after the amount of stuff in the home becomes overwhelming. It's as though the person must do the entire cycle of having little, then having too much, and then whittling it down to what's important. If there's too much NINE energy, this can become extreme. A person first hoards then discards most everything they have, almost preparing to move at any moment or leave the planet entirely.

If the energy of this number is too strong, you may find yourself:

- Overwhelmed by clutter and hoarding more and more stuff only to dump the stuff in fits of cleaning frenzies.

- Becoming so focused on health that you hide from the world to preserve the physical self.

- You focus solely on the spiritual, ignoring simple daily tasks like paying bills or doing laundry.

- You study, plan, and prepare but never really execute your plans.

CULTURAL MEANING

NINE is considered a fortunate number in most Asian countries. It is a Yang number and the Metal element (wealth and practicality). It is the "largest" number of the nine numbers, and it's considered the "emperor" of the numbers. Often Emperors of China wore robes decorated with nine dragons. In Chinese, Nine sounds like the word for 'longevity.' It is considered lucky and auspicious.

It is also considered lucky in the West because it is the highest of the single-digit numbers and, therefore, the best of the numbers.

The house number is 801
The energy is NINE (8+1=9)

A house like this shows a lot of creative energy which is related to the number NINE.

The decorative dentils show the love and craftsmanship that went into the house and emphasize the NINE energy.

Too much NINE energy can cause residents to horde or get overwhelmed with clutter. It would be good to trim away bushes and keep landscaping very tidy.

IF YOU WANT MORE NINE ENERGY:

- Display books in the home, frame and hang educational degrees, and display things important to you, such as family heirlooms and pictures.

- Have fruit trees in the yard or a vegetable garden.

- Hang religious symbols or spiritual artwork.

- Have a creative workshop or area of the home where you invent things or produce art.

IF YOU WANT LESS NINE ENERGY:

- Allow plants to be overgrown and fill in any gaps with a variety of plants.

- Keep lots of expensive toys like jet skis, go-carts, drones, and video game consoles.

- Add contrasting exterior trim to windows and doors, especially trim painted black.

- Inside, display organizing systems like bins, cubbies, or large entertainment centers.

HOW NINE IS WRITTEN

Originally, the number NINE was written more like a question mark without the dot at the bottom. It morphed into something that looked more like a THREE—and this brought confusion—then changed again into a THREE with a circle around it like our modern-day @ sign is a circle around an 'a'. Finally, it became the number we are familiar with today. This energy of its taking time to find its design is similar to the time it takes for NINE's energy to be felt in a home. The positive attributes of this number emerge only after months or even years in the house.

NINE can be seen as the reverse of the SIX, and where SIX is focused on nurturing the "child," NINE is out there taking care of the world. The NINE can be drawn starting from the top of the loop, in a sense looping and catching energy from heaven and then bringing it down to earth. Here we are taking all the ideas and beliefs we have collected and deciding what has value in our lives. Then what we don't need is discarded, and we focus on just what we need, as seen with the number ending on a single stroke drawn to the bottom.

The NINE can also be drawn starting with the bottom of the loop and continuing around like a spiral. Here we have more of a continuation energy. The spiral could keep going around and around. When a NINE is drawn in this fashion, it could suggest difficulty letting go of what is no longer needed but holding on just in case it's needed in the future.

THE HOUSE NUMBER FONT OF NINE:

If the NINE sits lower than the other numbers, it's viewed as more focused, stubborn in its ideas, and less willing to change. It can be intolerant and wish to avoid all new information and be capable of both deception and self-deception. If the NINE sits higher than the other numbers, it can have lofty ideals and be guided by a generous heart. However, too much of this energy can cause the person to give away what they needed themselves.

EXAMPLES OF NINE HOUSES

9–This is a lucky number for a house. Living in this house can bring opportunities for good health, long life, and happiness. Luck comes slowly at first, but builds and brings fortune with it. People become more mindful of what they do, say, and what they consume. Overtime spending is decreased, and savings are increased.

90–This adds the cosmic egg of potential to the mix, and when goals are clear, more opportunities come to the home. If the residents are undecided about their direction, there will still be opportunities, but some will not pan out, or they may experience "tests" and challenges to help them grow.

900–Here, opportunities and creativity abound. There's almost too much to do in one lifetime, let alone the time you're in the house. There's a need for discernment and judgment; otherwise useless pursuits eat away time.

9000–With this number, there can be so many paths to choose from it becomes overwhelming. Information is collected, but there's too much to process, and no decision is made, no direction is chosen. The focus turns inward, and residents can be consumed by taking care of health to the extent of foregoing happiness. Or they can be buried in stuff, not knowing how to let go or seeing the task of decluttering as overwhelming and so never really starting.

ZERO

While there may be a ZERO in the house number, no house number will add up to ZERO. There are some rare cases where the house number does start on ZERO, but most of the time, it's a number with other numbers.

ZERO is the state of nothingness, a place of beginning, of potential. Because it's the beginning, it's also the last point of the ending. So it's the space between the loss of something old and the starting of something new. For this reason, it can make things feel like they go on and on. As one cycle ends, the next begins, sometimes without having that space where we can think to change directions. Several ZEROs can mean cycle after cycle after cycle. Time passes, and it seems like we don't know where the time went, like being in a "groundhog's day" loop.

It's sometimes called the "egg of potentiality." This gives it positive energy when fertility or creativity is essential in the house. Inside this egg are all possibilities if you dream big enough. Let go of limitations, and you can find the resources to create anything.

If your house number begins with a ZERO, it can feel like things don't get off the ground because you don't know where to start. You have the joy of so many options, but you may not even know the first practical step to take. Everything then becomes a pleasant daydream, and nothing practical ever manifests.

ZERO's in the house number can mean a pause in progress on projects while you live in the house. This can be seen as a setback, but it's most useful to see it as a point to assess before moving forward. If the desire is always to be moving forward on a career path or financially, this energy can be challenging. But if it can be seen as a rest stop on the way to your goals, then it can either get you back on the right track or propel you forward on your path.

How ZERO is drawn: If your ZERO is a closed-loop, each ending brings a new beginning. If your ZERO loop is open, there can be a disconnect between an ending and a beginning. There can be the feeling that things have ended prematurely or that you need to begin things before you feel ready.

ZERO energy is continuous energy that goes on and on.

84935758 © creativecommonsstockphotos - Dreamstime.com

A round house or a driveway with a large circle emphasizes the ZERO energy. It can bring energy of fertility and creativity but too much ZERO energy will just spin you in circles never manifesting into something real.

9338560 © Ffennema – Dreamstime.com

Going Deeper

The root number of your house number is just the beginning of what you can learn about your house's energy. As I hinted before, you can take each number in your house number and read the complete energy of the "name" of the house. I wrote about this for many years in my blog.

For example, the number 27 can be read as "relationships are affected by beliefs." This could mean a range of things from political arguments in the home to the family, as a unit, shifting long-held spiritual beliefs. It might be the case that a family member changes religions or adopts a spiritual practice, which affects the other people in the household. If family members are aware of the energies that the house is adding to the mix, the challenges can be turned into opportunities.

If a person lives alone in a house with the number 27, their own beliefs could isolate them from others, and the acquiring of stuff can feel like a replacement for an intimate relationship. But over time, this number becomes quite beneficial as the root number NINE will bring happiness, long life, and prosperity. After a while, the resident(s) will start taking better care of their health, let go of unnecessary belongings, find more satisfaction in work and leisure time, and access opportunities for wealth.

Sometimes the order of the number is crucial. For example, the number 4321 can be thought of as a number that is decreasing. There will be loss in this house, a need to let go of things. That said, much of the loss will be things or relationships that were not serving your highest good. At the time, this may not be a comfort. After the loss, this house will become the place from which you launch your new life. The decreasing number represents the "countdown." This would be a difficult place to live for an extended period, but quite beneficial if you stay just a few years.

EXAMPLES OF HOUSE NUMBERS
THAT BEGIN WITH ZERO

I've only had a few clients who lived in homes with numbers that started on a ZERO. Several had strained marriages. It's difficult because the ZERO has trouble connecting. If the person divorced and stayed in the house, then the ZERO may affect the finances (making it difficult to accumulate money). It would be good to consider moving. One client built a house and started the number with ZERO in an attempt to hide. That's never a good sign. When you hide from the world, you miss out on all its benefits.

One client was moving into building 5, unit 8, but on the door, it was listed as 05-08. This number can make things very slow to start, with lots of spinning your wheels with no traction. It's pivotal with this energy to plan before taking any action. This number would imply a need to "plant then weed, plant some more and succeed."

Consider an apartment in building 8, unit 63. On the door is the number 08-63. The apartment number is the most important number, as it directly relates to the energy you live with. In this case, 08-63 would have been a great number if it didn't start on a ZERO. Beginning with a ZERO can cause you not to receive the resources and help needed to get things off the ground. Everything needs to be started from scratch, and many times things take much longer to get started than they should. If your house or apartment number begins with a ZERO, I suggest you decorate your entryway with egg-shaped art. Use things like egg-shaped stones, pictures of eggs, or decorated eggs and display them near your entryway. Eggs are round like a ZERO, but they offer the potential of food, life, and abundance. This can help mitigate the negative energy of the ZERO and help you capitalize on the positive energy of the rest of the number.

House Number Interpretations
—an abbreviated list

Of course, there are thousands and thousands of combinations of house numbers. There are too many to cover them all in this book. But over the years, I've interpreted many house numbers for clients. Here is a selection of interpretations I've done. If you are interested in having your house number interpreted, you can email me at DonnaStellhorn@gmail.com.

10A–When a letter is added to a house number, you need to convert the letter to a number and add it to the other numbers. In this case, "A" is the first letter of the alphabet, and so it's number 1. Interpreting this house number, we find a single-minded focus in the family, and that focus is interrupted occasionally by the ZERO, the cosmic egg of potentiality. This could be a pregnancy, a new business idea, or a new addition to the household like a roommate. There is a disruption for a while, in which you experience loss until focus returns.

House number 10A has a root number of TWO. 1+0+1=2. The overall energy of the house is about relating to others. This works well with the number itself, as the person or family in the house has a single goal or focus, which is then disrupted by the ZERO and then returns to a single focus. This ability to return to the focus is facilitated by the resident's relationship or partnership with the new person or thing coming into the house.

In the picture above, notice how the numbers are written. For this particular house number plaque, we see the unusual split in the ZERO, leaving a crack of light for something new to come in. The "A" also has breaks in the lines, allowing for new ideas and input to come into the household. This script for the numbers is particularly beneficial for this number.

13–suggests individuals can come together, pooling their talents to build a business. It's about how to take action and communicate with others. In a residence, this can be difficult energy, always having to let something go, but in a business, you're always trying to put something out into the world, which can work in your favor.

15–gives a sense of independence. This house will have many social activities, people visiting and parties. There will be a desire to renovate the house, and these renovations extend for a long time. Also, there will be an addition to the family. This may be a child, pet, or perhaps a relative will come to stay for an extended period. This house will attract a moderate to good amount of money.

Variations on the Number 13

This number 13 is drawn with the footed ONE and a simple THREE indicating stability and logical thinking can prevail in the house.

Here both the ONE and the THREE have a level top indicating a great deal of focus on tradition and sticking to the rules. The large bottom on the THREE can mean wealth is the goal.

Both the ONE and THREE stand on a point, ready to tip to one side or another in the moment. This could bring more risk taking or willingness to experiment.

16–the family will be self-reliant and successful; however, they can be weighed down with negative attitudes or miss opportunities due to onerous beliefs. It's a smart idea to examine beliefs carefully before launching big, important projects.

17–says focused action on your beliefs and ideas create money, power, and happiness.

18–this number will bring you prosperity and an overall sense of well-being. What will be required from you is to make yourself and your family the priority. It's the "charity starts at home" idea. Before you start giving anything away (time, energy, or money), think if someone at home needs it.

21–is about a couple unifying their goals, resulting in good communication, creativity, and attracting helpful friends.

22–with this number, we have different interpretations from the Western and Eastern schools of thought. In the West, we would say this is the master number of the grand builder, the one who can build a wonderful life. In Feng Shui, we would say this number will bring strong partnerships but lots of hard work and potential losses. It will be invaluable to both form and release partnerships. Have lots of friends and business associates, so when it's time to let go, you can release a minor partnership rather than a major one. It will be easy to collect too much stuff in this house (everything will come in twos), and too much clutter will stop the money flow. So releasing and letting go of stuff will help prosperity as well as relationships.

22A–has a strong emphasis on partnership. It will be necessary to share household tasks with others in the house or hire help. Because the house adds up to a FIVE, you may be drawn to change or renovate the home.

24–this number expresses hard work, but the family can be quite happy and content. Avoid having clutter, especially around the back of the house. It can block the expected opportunities.

25–in Feng Shui, it's an auspicious combination of yin and yang. It is a nice balanced number bringing a good relationship, lots of social opportunities, and strong spiritual connections.

28–is when two people (in a relationship or a business partnership) come together to bring a vision into life for profit. This results in a unified focus and facilitates building a life together.

31–can be good in that it will attract friends who love the authentic you. But this home has challenges, too. Over time there's a desire to see fewer and fewer people and devote oneself either to solitary hobbies or work. You may find you feel like you're connected to people because you call or text them, but friends need to be in your home often to offset this number's more difficult energy. A separation between public and private areas of the home is also important.

I suggest you always have the living room ready for guests and invite people to come over often. Then keep your bedroom private as a sanctuary for yourself. Also, I suggest you place something shiny gold near the back door, patio door, or in the kitchen. This could be a vase, bowl, or a religious statue. This will attract prosperity energy into the home, turning your challenges into gold.

33–is good energy, as it will give you many creative ideas and opportunities to collaborate, resulting in a home filled with love and prosperity.

34–the number 34 is about the family finding creative and innovative ways of doing career and business. This will lead to the residents receiving respect and recognition. This number means that some work is needed to achieve good communication within the home. It's important not to argue over differing opinions, but to be a united family focused on loving and supporting each other. Also, this house can attract clutter. It will always be necessary to release excess stuff; otherwise, you will find money is slow to accumulate. This is a valuable house for people who own their own business or work in teaching, publishing, writing, advertising, the travel industry, or the legal professions.

In the example above, the four is extremely open and unformed. This number 34 could bring a lot of creative ideas from the 3 that don't manifest into practical action because of the unformed 4.

35–is about creative ideas and connecting with interesting people. Making bold choices leads to prosperity and happiness.

In the example above, we see the number 36 in a very protective font. The flat top of the three gives you a "level head" and so you're not easily deceived. Additionally, the top of the six almost touches the bottom loop and so it closes off any outside influences. So the experience would be a very tightknit family.

37–This can be quite good, especially for spiritual, religious, teachers, or lawyers. It's essential in this home to be united. Arguments within the home will bring resentment and block money opportunities.

41–is about working hard to reduce things down to the simplest form. This is a fine choice for people who are into downsizing or living simpler lives. This is also a good house to run a business involving consulting, translating, tutoring, or personal organizing. If a business is run in this house it can offset the negative energy of the FOUR and the home will be the center of parties and fun. It will also have prosperity.

42–this number means hard work ahead, and there will be a need to offset loss by getting rid of excess clutter. There will be a desire to work on relationships, and you will grow closer to those in the home. You will become more united in your goals and ultimately feel happy with the results. Be ready to release and let go of anything that doesn't benefit you, and new opportunities will come to replace what you have let go of.

In the example above, the 42 has a closed 4 and a very blocky 2. This font is very mathematical, practical, and no nonsense. The people in this house work hard and don't give a lot of time for frivolous activities. Romance and fun are probably not on the agenda. And letting go of things only happens when it makes practical sense.

43–this number means "hard work brings growth." It's only through hard work and having a good plan that you can prosper. I suggest putting up a vision board or have your goals written and posted where you can see them often. Sometimes, this number's energy can cause people to forget about their goals and just end up working hard. That said, this home would be ideal for a writer, publisher, minister, lawyer (especially one who advocates for the public good), or one involved in humanitarian efforts.

44–is a master number that does take a little finesse to get right. With any master number, you can get caught in the lower vibration, in this case, two FOURs. This number can mean hard work, but it also can bring prosperity. Be careful not to let any garbage collect for too long in your apartment, but always take it downstairs at least every other day. If you discard something often, then the 44 will not take something from you. It would be good to house a business in this location, especially one that deals with potential losses such as insurance, counseling, or home security.

45–in Feng Shui, there are ways to mitigate the energy of the unlucky FOUR. This number is lucky because it's a combination of yin and yang and adds up to NINE. So what is lost through the FOUR is balanced and harmonized by the FIVE. This is one of the better numbers that contains a FOUR. This number means that there will be many opportunities through work and effort, resulting in happiness and financial prosperity. With this number, it's important to remember to do the work first, and then the rewards come.

Think of chores before TV, homework before play. Do the hard stuff before doing the easy stuff, and your success will build. What seems hard at first will become easier and easier. In addition, with all houses that contain a FOUR in the number, it's always helpful to work out of the home or have a home business. This channels the FOUR energy into something positive and creates wealth.

46–the number 46 is a bit of a mixed blessing. The number means that the people living there will work hard to build savings and good relationships. Things will improve. However, this number can reveal a person in the family who is entirely selfish, which can throw off the household's harmony. This energy can be improved by having a business in the home or decorating the home with strong materials like slate, stone, or brick. I also suggest you take a family portrait and frame it in a stone frame (sandstone or onyx would work well.) Place this picture in the living room or family room. This will help balance the energy and bring financial stability to the household.

47D–Here, we have house number 47 unit D, which gives additional FOUR energy. This number would read—hard work and loss may come from beliefs or personal rules leading to a family that closes ranks and relies on each other. The root number is SIX. D is the fourth letter of the alphabet. 4+7+4=15. 1+5=6.

In the picture above, the number is written with a closed 4, suggesting plans are solid and difficult to change even if circumstances change. The 7 has a hook on the top, revealing a desire to grab hold of concepts and ideas. The upper case D shows strength and resolve, giving the FOUR energy more importance.

52–is about choices (perhaps in career or just ideas) leading a couple or family to embrace strong beliefs. These beliefs can be religious or political. There can be memorable parties in this house, where people come together to share great ideas. I suggest Feng Shui money cures for this home, as this number doesn't attract much money.

In the example above, the numbers are written in a very stylized, heavy font. This can bring an excess of energy. Changes in the lives of the family members are bigger than expected—parties last longer, beliefs are more intense. There may be issues with hoarding or weight gain as everything in the house could be done to excess.

53—is about creating change and following a different path while collaborating with others. This number supports people who network or have a large group of friends. The energy encourages risk-taking and following your instincts. The issue with this number is when you want things to be stable, the energy is disruptive and creates change. Feng Shui cures can help stabilize this energy.

56—is a positive number. It brings variety, change, and fun for the family. This may be a very social home, the hub of the neighborhood where you are visited by neighbors and friends of your children. You can accomplish much in this home, but the energy is wasted if there are no clear goals. Goals need to be agreed upon by the family (not separate goals for each person), and action needs to happen weekly or monthly towards each goal.

57—brings an energy of creativity, cooperation, and creative ideas.

In the example above, the top part of the number is short and the bottom half is exaggerated. This can indicate that there is less thought and more action. There may be more emphasis on the physical or material than there is on the intellectual or spiritual. On the other hand, these two numbers seem to be dancing together. And this could indicate great cooperation and creativity for the people living in the house.

58–is about changing many of the ways you're doing things, and through those changes creating more money and success. However, the root number is FOUR, an energy-requiring you to let go of something in the process. You may find every time you get a pay increase, it's important to allocate that money to savings otherwise you may find another bill pops up and drains the account. The energy of this house number works well for people who work on a contract basis or have a variable income.

59–is often about making choices and having opportunities to take you and your family in very different directions. Overtime, finances, and health improve, and this can be a happy place. This is an excellent place to have parties and get together with friends. The challenging part of this number is that members of the family can go separate ways. To create family togetherness, display family portraits in the living room and dining room.

59A–Here is another example of a house number with the addition of a letter. This adds the number ONE to the energy of the number. This number reads–Change and creativity lead to wisdom and understanding. This allows the family to act in a loving and unified manner. The root number is SIX. 5+9+1=15. 1+5=6.

In the picture above, notice how the number is written, so the "A" is much smaller than the number. Emphasis will be on the other numbers rather than the ONE energy the "A" brings. This tones down the focus and self-interest often seen with the number ONE. Additionally, the 59 is written with a ball at the end of each number, bringing in more creative energy and style. This can suggest more art or design could go on in the house.

63–this is a positive number. This energy will keep you in constant motion. This number implies that you need to remain a cohesive family unit, a united front when tackling the challenges the world brings you. It also shows that when you need more money in your life, the best way to stimulate the energy is to remove clutter. The more you get rid of, the more that can flow in.

65–is about embracing change on lots of levels and using opportunities to design the life you want.

67–is about a family with strong spiritual values working hard to help each other. As the root number of this house is FOUR, it's a good idea to consciously let go otherwise there can be losses. Having a business in the home, especially one that deals in inventory, or service businesses that help people through losses, would help bring stable, prosperous energy.

70– there's a lot of creative potential with this number. The people living in the home will likely do something creative. You may want to add feng shui cures to attract prosperity as the number itself is not a money number. The people in the house will also have strong beliefs. If those beliefs limit the things that you want to attract, you might want to look at changing your thoughts about this.

Here the ZERO represents the egg of potentiality and can be the key to unlock success.

75–is lucky for teachers, writers, people in advertising, law students and lawyers, religious leaders, and community leaders. There can be arguments in the home as this number can make residents very opinionated. It's good to have a lot of books in this house. This helps channel the energy in a more positive direction. It's also a good idea to clear this home once every couple of months to keep money energy flowing.

76–this number means respect for various opinions and views within the house. It's said that if there are quarrels, "only bad luck follows." The problem with living in a house that adds up to a four is you need to be constantly watchful of slipping into negative energy. You can stabilize this energy by adding hard materials to the home, such as granite, brick, and steel. Also, it helps to work at home, either for a company or in your own business.

In the example above, the seven looks like a flag blowing in the breeze. The people living in the house may "plant a flag" to clearly state their beliefs. They may fly a literal flag for their country or to announce their favorite sports team. The eight is larger on the bottom than the top indicating more of an interest in the material. So this combination is about a belief system that leads to material benefits and overall this helps the household.

In general, the number 81 is a good number. It indicates that the family could manifest money and power by having a unified goal and over time, the household would experience happiness and prosperity. But in the example above we see both the 8 and the 1 standing on points. They are easy to topple over and so the energy is not stable but comes and goes.

83–means that money and creativity combine to bring positive results.

84–is quite positive for business. In a home, it can be difficult because it is such a strong business number. You may want to run a business from your home to offset the energy. This number will ask you to have big dreams and work hard to manifest those dreams. The number FOUR is going to try to take something from you each month. I suggest you channel the "ending energy" of the FOUR into a humanitarian cause. Place a bowl near the back or side door and each week add a few coins. At the end of the month, donate the money to charity. This will help balance the energy.

88–is a fortunate number. This number brings prosperity and long life. However, this number does not help your relationship if you have a history of arguing. Communication will be key in this home.

93–this number is very positive and brings abundance and good family communication over time. But be watchful about excessive worry in the home. This can reduce the positive energy of this number.

99–is about gathering everything that comes to you, deciding what is useful, and discarding the rest—and doing this over and over and over. For example, a person who shops too much may find living in this energy brings a total change in how they spend money and what they spend money on. They can go from hoarder to minimalist. Or a person who has many acquaintances, but no true friends could find themselves ending many relationships until only the best people are left. As one category is cleaned up, another will become urgent. The number brings spiritual and emotional growth, helping remove blocks to success. Remaining in a house of this energy will bring prosperity after a time, as you will find many of the blocks you've had in your life disappear. So this number is challenging at first, but gets better.

101–The number 101 will bring money and lots of opportunity for independence. But this is a very difficult number for being in a relationship. It attracts two powerful, opinionated people who rarely see eye-to-eye. For this number, I suggest you place a picture of a bridge (one where you can see both ends of the bridge) in your bedroom or family room. This will represent a way to connect with your partner and anyone else you want to have a relationship with. Stuffed

107–The number 107 is a little tricky. The individual numbers can be difficult, but the number's overall energy is positive. It would be beneficial to have the family come together regularly for meals, meetings, game night, etc. If family members don't come together, there can be quarrels, and children may be rebellious. But after a short while living there, you will find the house brings you more prosperity, and with it, more happiness.

109–is about individuals with firm opinions, finding they need to let go of those ideas, start over, build new beliefs, and collect what matters. This results in the individual becoming stronger, more confident, more self-assured. This is a suitable house for people studying meditation, mindfulness, minimalism, and art of all kinds. This is also a place where there will be positive fertility energy. The caution here is when ending on a NINE, you can collect a lot of material possessions and then have trouble letting go. It can also be a place you have trouble leaving. If this is a temporary house, you will have to do some Feng Shui cures when you want to move.

114–an unlucky number, causing you to focus on hard work and loss instead of all the gains. The gains still happen, but the residents have trouble feeling the joy. To reduce unlucky energy and to attract positive energy, decorate the house with lots of things made of stone (like granite countertops, slate floors, etc.). The hardness felt in the home will be in the surfaces, rather than the feelings of the people living there.

115–is about very independent people coming together to create a new path and change. This home is right for teachers, writers, politicians, religious leaders, and thought leaders. You can add Feng Shui cures to bring prosperity.

116–is two independent people learn to take care of each other, and the results bring prosperity to the home.

117–is a lucky number that means several like-minded individuals come together for both a physical and spiritual union. This is great for a family. This house will attract good friends and profitable business opportunities. However, sometimes with this house, there will be the temptation to be overly critical, especially of each other in the household. I suggest you display musical instruments in the living room or family room. This will mitigate the quarreling energy. Then the lucky energy of this house will be available to attract prosperity.

119–is the energy of diverse individuals blending together for physical, spiritual, and material reasons. Evolved souls will find this home inspires them to great ideas and important community service. This home will bring happy relationships for the residents and no worries about money after a few years.

120–is suitable for a person who wants to be in a love relationship or create business partnerships. But there's a warning when a house number ends on zero. You must be willing to let go of something to gain something. For example, a person must let go of the positive aspects of being single to become a person in a committed relationship. Or when you buy something, you need to release something, or else the house just fills up with stuff.

121–is about individuals coming together to act as a unit, but this takes hard work, compromise, and some will not get what they want (loss). This can be a challenging number for some families, but if you are already a tight unit and you work at family relations, you can grow a great deal in this home. Your work ethic will be key. It would be good to limit distractions such as television or video games. Focus everyone on working together for common goals.

126–means individuals with a strong sense of their value and worth connect with like-minded people to form good and loving relationships. These bring happiness and prosperity to the household. What's important here is always to maintain that sense of your own identity. If you sacrifice yourself for others, then the whole chain of positive energy breaks down. Otherwise, this is a good number for a happy, prosperous household.

135–is a strong number sequence that brings you the energy of building and growing. This home will be a very powerful one. However, you may find the energy is so strong it's sometimes hard to rest. Creating a balanced energy inside the home will be very important. This home needs soft furnishings and lots of curved lines. It needs some dark colors, peaceful sounds, and a place to meditate. In the home office, focus on attracting the money energy through decor. Make it bright with a solid desk and art that depicts mountains and waterfalls. This will help you capitalize on the strong prosperity energy.

145–is a good number for a person in business who's open to change or a person in a leadership position who is looking for new opportunities. The difficulty here is between the concept and what it takes to make the concept a reality. There can be losses related to investment money or time. There is a need to let go of preconceived notions. This number can be challenging for a family if there are selfish people in the household.

148–can be a very positive number if you work with the energy. This means "if you stay independent, you are sure to prosper." To find success in this home, avoid debt, build a good savings account, and stay out of questionable business partnerships. If you do these things, you are sure to prosper.

161–is about independence and self-care. There is prosperity possible in this house. If you are focused on being independent, you can have success here.

162–This number expresses a unified household where love and partnership are encouraged and even celebrated, and brings prosperity and longevity. The root number is NINE. 1+6+2=9. This is a good number for a happy residence where there is love and acceptance in the home.

In the picture above, you can see the font used on this number is unusual. The 1 stands on a point rather than a solid base. So the emphasis on self-interest is less, or it can be swayed through negotiation. The 6 is not a closed-loop, so it's open to accepting outside support, and new people can join the household. The 2 has a wavy base showing that relationships can change over time and yet still be steady and loving. The number six and the number two are actually touching. They show more unity. So individuality is not as valued in this household as is family and the partnership.

164–this house has an energy of single-minded determination to work hard. This hard work brings success with big goals but difficulty coping with day-to-day tasks. In other words, you will need help to take care of this house. Otherwise, long-term success will not be easy. If you live alone, get a house cleaning service and a gardener. If you live there with family members, make sure to assign everyone chores.

165–with this house number, there may be a lot of scattered energy, everyone doing their own thing with little regard for the others in the house. One person can pull the family together, a strong personality in the house, bringing everyone back together into a cohesive family unit. In this home, you might have meals together and dinner parties. This will encourage the energy of joy and prosperity. This is also an ideal house for writers and creative types. Overall, this is a good house number unless only one person shoulders all the responsibilities for the whole family.

166–gives the energy of wanting to take care of others, even to the point of not taking good care of yourself. It can be right for a family if they take care of each other. But it can be challenging if one person in the household takes on the role of taking care of all the others. You can work yourself into exhaustion without feeling any support or recognition for what you are doing. You will want to set some boundaries. You can also represent boundaries by fencing in the property.

171–is an energy of individuality expressed through writing, art, speaking, and teaching. This house will help you solidify your beliefs, and you could do well in business if the business involves information, ideas, or teaching. Overall, this is a lucky number; however, there is a sense of separation in relationships, not meaning that you will lose your partner but that each person in the relationship will have very separate lives, only really feeling togetherness when talking and sharing ideas.

172A–adds up to the master number 11. The people who live there will enjoy a happy marriage and, if they plan ahead, will easily achieve their goals. If it's a rental property, this place will rent to someone looking for love, and marriage is likely while living in the house.

172B–this number encourages good communication and a happy family life. This is positive energy for a home business. Overall, you will become a closer family in this home.

174–this house number is difficult. This is a better number for business than relationships. It says individual effort, vision, and hard work combine to bring success. But it warns that you need to keep the clutter out of the house because clutter, in this case, will block money flow. Everyone in the house may be so focused on career or school they don't notice or appreciate the family around them. You can live in this house happily by having a weekly family meeting. Bring everyone together to help prepare and serve the evening meal, and that will bring you all closer together. Or display family photos that show happy times when everyone was together.

202 –adds up to a 4, meaning you need a lot of structure and to stay free of clutter, or else this number can bring a lot of hard work or even losses. There's a balance to the number having a TWO on either side of the ZERO. This can cause relationships to go through a shift but come back, perhaps even stronger, and better than before. This number is very much about having balance in your life. This is the sweet with the sour, the lesson, and the gift. There may be ups and downs, but each down is followed by an up.

205–is about two people in partnership but who also have very separate lives or life paths. This is an intellectual or educational number and lends its energy to teachers, writers, and people who travel for work.

214- is a bit challenging as house numbers go. It starts well with two people or multiple people coming together and being of one mind. Residents live in harmony and agreement. But there's much hard work in their lives, and they can get stuck in rigid thinking or ideas that don't create prosperity or ease. To attract financial success, have a business in the home (especially businesses dealing with money or financial planning) or have an area dedicated to finance and investment. Keep clutter away from the front door so that new opportunities can come in easily. Review goals monthly to make sure you're not putting a lot of time and energy into projects that are not going anywhere.

217–the house number 217 shows a couple of one mind spreading their thoughts, influence, and words into the community. This is a good number for two people who work in teaching, writing, communication, politics, or spiritual professions. If one person is extreme in their views, the other family members may be very influenced and everyone in the household comes to believe the same thing.

220–This house will allow you to create the future you want if you take a few precautions. First, you must have a clear vision of what you want and use that vision to guide your actions. 22 is a master number, but when it's coupled with the zero, it can erase progress if you're not clear on what you want. Write down your goals and post them where you can see them. If you find you are working too hard or if gains seem to be slipping away, it may be because you've forgotten what's on your list of goals.

223– In this house, you'll focus on relationships with your partner and other family members. This will result in better communication and understanding. The difficulty could be if one person has a strong desire to be right versus being happy. With this number, you need to set ground rules from the beginning to form a true partnership. Each person needs to contribute to the wellbeing of the home. If not, arguments will happen. To quell argumentative energy, hang or display a musical instrument such as a flute in the family room or dining room.

234–even though this number ends in a 4, you can find success in this home. This number gets larger with each digit, so your bank accounts will grow. This number means that like-minded people pool their resources to achieve their goals. I suggest you have very clear goals in this house, so the positive energy doesn't go to waste.

In the example above, we see the number 236 with the number 3 set lower than the other two numbers. This means that its energy is more based in the physical and material world. So while the number 236 would normally be that a couple, through collaboration, creates things that benefit the family. Now what is created may be more physical or material. This could cause the family to cut corners to make an extra dollar. Or that collaborations are done with people of questionable intentions.

In the example above, the number two is closed off. This would indicate that it's a very insulated family. That there is not a lot of connection with the outside world. Normally this number would read as a couple, through collaboration, creating prosperity and longevity. But this closed off two may curtail collaboration or may cause the family not to share anything outside of the family.

271–is the energy of two people with like-minded beliefs and ideals becoming focused on a single goal. You will find you do best in this home when you openly examine your beliefs and challenge what's not working for you. Often we are limited by our thinking rather than something external. In this home, you can remove obstacles to what you want by shifting how you see and interact with the world.

279–is good for promoting a healthy, happy home life. This number will bring you both closer as a couple and strengthen your beliefs (spiritually as well as mentally and emotionally). It can also bring prosperity and luck.

In the example above, the eight is flanked by two of the number 2. The number 2 is written with a wavy base. This could indicate ongoing changes in the relationship. The number itself almost appears to be one person standing between two partners. Additionally 282 adds up to the number 3 which could indicate a third person.

303–Numbers with the ZERO in the center can cause instability in money flow and career. People who work in seasonal businesses, for instance, have a period of high activity followed by a lull followed by high activity can do well in this energy. This number, 303, has balance and potential for prosperity if the residents are creative and enjoy collaborating with others.

304–is about a home that promotes good communication, creative ability, and lots of ideas, but most of these ideas are either discarded or lost because everyone is caught up in day-to-day activities. This number can cause people to have lives so busy they never get around to doing the things they enjoy. It's essential in this household to have clear goals (you might even want to post them in the kitchen) and every day do something towards them. If you want to add children to the household, this number, 304, is positive. If there are blocks, the people in the house feel additional children will be too much work or cost too much money. This is a good house for writers, teachers, people who travel for work, politicians, and those in legal professions. It's beneficial to have books, computers, and musical instruments in this house.

307–is lucky, but it's not consistent luck, especially at first. With this number, the residents need to be cautious that their own rules or

limiting beliefs don't keep them from prosperity. Opportunities that come will have
a setback or pause before manifesting into
something positive.

311–brings communication and independence
in the home. This is a good home for parties,
and it could end up being the social hub with
your friends. You will receive quite a few opportunities in this house, especially in the area
of career. There will be more harmony if each
child has a space of their own (even if it's one
room separated by a curtain). If you're looking
for love, Feng Shui cures would be needed, as
this number is often happier being single than
in a relationship.

312–is where creative ideas need to be blended
and honed into a single goal or principle, and
then action results in success. The challenge
is to find common ground between various
ideas or family members. It can be that people
in the household want different (conflicting)
things. But it can also be that you have conflicting ideas, such as wanting to get a new job
but feeling uncomfortable about interviewing.
Displaying family photos can help bring harmony to the household.

314–is people coming together with creative
ideas. Hard work is needed to be done in a unified
fashion, and this brings success and prosperity. The best businesses under this number have
an inventory, so there's a flow of products in
and out. Also, this home is good for businesses

where you "lose" customers because they no longer need your services, like a daycare where the children become old enough to go on to school or a tutoring service where the students graduate and no longer need your services.

316–This number has religious significance if you are Christian. You can use Christian symbols to bring blessings into your home. The energy of this number brings positive communication of ideas. It attracts love and nurturing to the family.

323–is an apt number for partnerships of all kinds. This is excellent energy for people who work in creative or communication fields. Prosperity is probable when the residents work with others rather than working alone.

324–despite the number FOUR in the house number, this could be a delightful home. Creativity and working on good communication causes the people in the house to become closer, helping them work together. It would be good to take a few bags of extra stuff to charity every few months to offset the FOUR energy. But overall, this is a house that will have prosperity and wisdom.

336–is an exciting, creative number that brings wonderful social opportunities.

354–is about teamwork, people with different skills coming together to make a better life (or at least a different life). Place or hang a pair of wooden flutes in the living room or kitchen to create open and harmonious communication.

367–This number suggests creative ideas that come together with others (who may live within the house or be outsiders) to form loving bonds and bring forth new ideas and concepts.

In the picture above, the 3 and 6 are written in a conventional form and without any flourish. But the 7 has a small line through it, indicating there may be a separation between thoughts and practical action. This could be emphasized by the root number also being SEVEN. This increases the SEVEN energy and may cause the residents to focus on gathering information rather than putting the information to use.

392– brings many opportunities in both business and relationships. This can be a house filled with laughter and joy.

408–is a good number for a person who wants business success and works in a field that requires creativity, communication, and cooperation. Prosperity will come slowly, so be patient. Perseverance is key to success with this energy.

422–this energy may cause you to have to work hard at first, but with hard work, you will get some fantastic results. The temptation here will be to think that organizing will solve problems where you'll need bold action and calculated risks to attract the bounty of what this number can bring. Meet often together, as a family, so that everyone has the same goals and discuss how to take action.

433–is suitable for a person who lives alone and wants to stay that way. If you want a relationship, consider adding feng shui cures like pairs of objects or the color red.

435–is good for a couple who is willing to work at good communication. Over time this house will attract a lot of social opportunities and good friends.

437–is for a family that likes adventure and fun. The best energy for this number is doing things outside your comfort zone. If you "rough it," you'll use up the FOUR energy. So you might have antique appliances or not use the heater unless it's really cold.

439–is for a family that has strong beliefs or religious convictions. It's ideal if the religion has rules or restrictions that you must follow to adhere to your faith.

441–despite having two FOURs, 441 adds up to 9, bringing health, wealth, and happiness. It's necessary to stick to routines and follow good health habits. Over time, you'll find that you're happy in this house.

450–hard work and change (being open and flexible to opportunities) will bring prosperity and longevity. It will take several years to happen. If you plan to stay in this house for a long time, the energy of this house can benefit you and the family.

483– can bring hard work and some loss. But there can be gains in prosperity and friendships, leading to feeling loved and cared for. This is a good number for moving towards retirement. The loss of energy could be used to end the job. There will be hard work here too, which might be the upkeep of the house, but a better way to use it would be to do charity work or help in the community.

501–is a lively number, and changes in the home may be needed before things run smoothly. There may be some setbacks during projects expressed by the ZERO in the center of the number. This number is good for communication and intellectual growth. There will be many opportunities, but you must be very discerning about your time and resources. You might be very determined to do projects that are not actually worth the time, money, and energy.

505–can be an exciting energy—unfortunately, it's not a peaceful number. This energy is about one adventure after another, one party after another, one decision after another, one challenge after another. To bring good luck, you need always to make a decision, don't hesitate when a choice needs to be made. I suggest you hang pictures of a sailing ship in your home. This is to represent a safe vehicle to carry you and your family through any rough waters. This will also represent opportunities for wealth and success.

508–you will have excitement in this house. When there is a zero at the center of a number, you have an interruption in energy flow. You may have a line on a new job, and the interviews are proceeding just fine, then silence—no one is returning your calls, and no one is calling you. Your reaction might be to give up and change directions. But instead, the best course is to stay the course and just wait out the interruption. To mitigate this energy, you want to avoid having anything in the house's center that resembles a hole or a block. A spiral staircase would be an example of an object that is "drilling a hole." A large stone fireplace in the center of the house would be an example of a block. I suggest you add flowers, plants, or a fish tank to the center of the house to bring energy and help shorten interruptions.

513–is a strong number that brings creativity, flexibility, and change. Overall, this number brings the challenge of discernment. This means each person in the house will decide what is important and what is not. The things or ideas that are not important will be discarded. While this process takes some time, it is very beneficial and ultimately leads to wealth and happiness.

559- will create energy of change and bring opportunities. The residents would do well by throwing parties and other social events. Most of the focus connected with this number will be around making choices. This house will probably require some changes or renovations. There will be situations where you can choose what's best for you. The lesson of this house is that "not making a choice is still a choice." Don't avoid decisions. The nine in the number will lead to prosperity and success. So as you learn to make better decisions, more success will come. There's one caveat of this house, and that is that 5+5+9 gives us the energy of the number ONE. This is great for independent thinking. However, this can take its toll on a relationship if one person makes all the decisions or if all the responsibilities are put on one person's shoulders. It will be essential to have regular family meetings and do what you can to stay connected.

606–this number brings a mix of blessings and challenges. When things seem to be going your way, opportunities suddenly dry up and disappear only to reappear in a different form. The secret to prospering in this location is to realize missed opportunities will come along again (that includes relationships). To gain benefits in this house, write down your list of goals and wishes, and place them near the front door. Try not to hold on to opportunities that seem to be disappearing but allow them time to reappear.

640–can be a good money number though it says that career may be more important to people who live in the house than family relations. It would be good to have a business in the home and work on it together. It's also vital to willingly let go of things in your life, or else this number can create some losses. Letting go of excess clutter and things you don't need will help with this energy. Focus on making money together as a family, and you'll have success.

707–is two people on opposite sides of an idea or ideology (like one democrat and one republican) with no meeting in the middle. This would be okay if you live alone, but it could be challenging for a couple. This is also a good number for a staff writer or journalist who has deadlines for their work.

723–is an excellent number for communication and communication-related careers. It is a creative energy. With this number, you need to work with others to find the full potential of the opportunities.

752–there will be lots of discussion about beliefs, goals, and the direction the family should take for the future in this home. Some of these discussions will be fun and lively, and some will not be as people will express their opinions strongly. There may be many changes in this home, including renovations but also career changes. To create more harmony in this home and to help you achieve what you want for your family, I suggest adding a musical instrument to the living room or family room. This could be a piano, harp, guitar, or the traditional Feng Shui flutes.

845–is about powerful goals and big ambitions requiring much work and effort, leading to exciting, unexpected results. Over a long time, there will be success, abundance, and longevity in this home.

899–is the energy of prosperity and power that goes on and on and on.

914–brings the need to work hard and let go of things that don't serve you. But with this energy, you can put plans into motion and accomplish more. Make a list of things that you are willing to let go of (bad job, bad habits, bad boyfriends, or whatever) and a second list of what you want. This will help deal with the FOUR energy and create changes you want.

917–is a very positive number, as long as you don't end up making a lot of rules for yourselves. Dogmatic rules or restrictions in this house will block prosperity.

952–is about collecting everything into a house (the people, things, information, etc.) and then trying to sort through it all to find what is useful and valuable. As you do, you will find your tastes change, and you become interested in other things. But over time, the energy of the house becomes more balanced and harmonious. The people in the home grow more philosophical and spiritual. This is a good house for writers, teachers, and travelers. Be careful not to accumulate too much clutter, as this will block opportunities.

962–this is a house number that will give you lots of friends and a family that grows while you grow closer together as a couple. There can be prosperity, and it will be vital that you do not give all your money away but keep some (or perhaps most) for yourselves and your retirement. Be watchful of frittering money away on immediate wants rather than investing for the future.

1049–can bring the desire to be social over doing most anything else. You will meet a lot of new people with this number. The focus will be on other people. Living alone in this residence will be difficult. Live with family, roommates, or pets to shift the energy to the positive.

1057–this energy has its challenges. This is a home where family members would come and go, moving in and moving out. There may be arguments in the home based on political or religious differences. Having a business in the home would help a lot to quell the unrest. Also, I would suggest a round dining table. This would help balance the energy and create more family harmony.

1303–brings a high level of activity to the house nearly all the time, not just your family but others (neighbors and friends) may be involved too. There can also be occasional interruptions of income. To guard against that, put off expensive renovation projects until you've been in the house a few years. Place stacks of coins on windowsills (stack them in three's or five's and use quarters, half dollars, or dollar coins). This can help bring money from more than one source to the home.

1311–has a lot of independent energy to it and can cause people to take more chances. Overall, this number is positive as it represents independent thinking people coming together to take care of one another.

1345–can be trying, but it also has a blessing with it. If you grew up with the idea of "eat your vegetables, then you can have dessert," you will be fine in this energy. But if you're a "dessert first" person, this energy can create struggle. Over time there will be growth, but it will take discipline and staying on a schedule.

1429–is an individual or several individuals with strong opinions and a strong work ethic bonding with others to create health, wealth, and happiness. The issue is that results can be more theory rather than practice. The challenge in this house is you may have the intuitive flash to invest in something, and your intuition proves correct, but you forgot to buy the stock. Or you have an invention in mind and are disappointed years later when you find someone else starts selling it. You can do some Feng Shui changes to make this energy more practical, but it also helps to be mindful of it. Have the inspiration but then take action as soon as possible.

1444–This is a number where you have to work hard to get the results you want. Living in this energy can cause you to want or need a second or even third job. Relationships may blur into business partnerships draining the romance from the relationship. I would recommend clearing as much clutter as possible (this will let money flow in more easily.) Have a lot of glass in the house, such as mirrors, windows, and glass furniture. This will help reduce the energy of the number FOUR and ease your workload. It would also help to have hard surfaces such as granite countertops, slate floors or other things made out of stone.

1526–is about some very independent people coming together in one family to have good relationships and care for each other. That said, it will take a bit of time for this to all work out, and during the transition, there may be some arguments and hurt feelings. It would be helpful for all of you to be empathetic with each other and work together. This is a suitable house for social activities, laughter, and fun. This is not a strong wealth number, so I recommend placing Feng Shui cures to accumulate money.

1587–has an energy of individuals coming into a house and shifting that relationship into a strong family unit. This would be a fine home for a blended family.

1593– new ideas are assessed and analyzed, resulting in new expansion, positive communication, and financial growth. If new ideas are not tested and updated, there can be stagnation. In this home, person-to-person communication and strategic partnerships will give you the most prosperity in the quickest time. There is also a party aspect to this number. Being social in this home will add to your happiness and success.

1594–shows a home where many renovation projects will take place. This home will not do well with clutter, so it's important to be always in the process of letting go of things that are no longer needed. This energy will inspire lots of independence in both adults and children, which can be good but can end up with the family feeling disconnected. I suggest a family portrait displayed in the living room or dining room to bring family unity. I also suggest running a home business out of this house. This will help change the challenging aspects into prosperity energy.

1706–says that if the family agrees on most matters, there will be happiness in this household. The ZERO in the number does mean there can be setbacks before there's success. Be prepared for some delays and have patience.

1750–means a very opinionated person learns to change their mind and consider other ideas. This will either lead to business success, or if there's no business, it will lead to letting go of outdated beliefs.

1905–expresses a focus on determining what's necessary for the family and what should be discarded. In this house, if you hold on to clutter, you will block opportunities. If you hold on too long to anything, it may be taken from you (that's the zero in the number), so regularly remove clutter and toss excess stuff. Positive things will happen in this home over time.

1914–means independent thinking people gather many ideas and things and then slowly decide what has value and what should be discarded. The results are general prosperity and good health. If things are not discarded and clutter takes over the house, it will eat away at the luck, and there will be losses in other areas.

1920–means "an independent person gathers resources together (including money) to establish good relationships and work/life balance." This is a good number–until you want to move. It's the ZERO at the end of this number that can cause problems. The ZERO can make it difficult to leave a situation or let go of anything. The house may fill with stuff, children may stay for a long, long time, or if you want to leave a relationship, you may have trouble doing so.

2158–shows people in a strong partnership in the beginning and becoming more individualistic as time goes on. This house will focus more on fun and business than family (which could work if you plan on having no kids or if kids have already left the nest). This house has an underlining energy that focuses the residents on spiritually. The energy may give you a desire to stand up for your faith or political leanings.

2207–this is a solid relationship number. This energy will bring you closer together at first; then, for a time, differences will need to be worked out for the relationship to continue. It will be necessary to air differences often so that no resentment builds. I suggest you hang flags or mobile to bring more ease and happiness to your home. Hang them in the living room, bedroom or on the front porch.

2371–shows people in a growing family need to listen to one another to manifest happiness and prosperity. This home requires open communication with those living in the house. Secrets and stubbornly wanting to be right will block prosperity. It's a good idea to have family dinners together and promote a lot of open communication around the dinner table.

2450A–means a couple works hard at creating a long-term relationship while feeling very independent of each other. It's possible that the family comes together only for special occasions but mostly pursues individual interests.

2790–brings long life and prosperity.

2811 is about people coming together to create prosperity and happiness, yet feeling strongly independent and having their own goals and dreams. The results are good when communication is positive, open, and truthful. If there's lying or concealment, then prosperity energy will be diminished.

2813– brings good energy for a couple or a family with focused ambitions for success and wealth. Together they can unite their talents and energies to create new roads to their chosen goals. The challenge in this house is to assess opportunities rather than trying to take all opportunities carefully. Try new things but don't scatter your energies.

3210–has the energy of reducing things until they are no more. This is a good house for weight loss but a difficult house for accumulating money. It's a good residence for getting rid of clutter, a difficult house for keeping a job. It's a proper house for selling a business, a difficult house growing and maintaining a business. Place a bowl or open vase by the back door to catch energy before it leaves the house.

3272–is about many connected people (the family, extended family, or maybe a wider circle of friends) coming together to share ideas and help each other. This results in having new opportunities and choices. This can be a lively house with many parties. This can be a home where many children are playing, good discussions happen between adults, and there is lots of creativity.

3414–is a good number for people who are organized and love their work. It's perfect for people with professions in teaching, finance, construction, or sales. Money will be a little tight the first year but improve every year after. The challenge with this number is that one person in the family ends up doing most of the household work, or work duties can get very split (so a person who does work outside the home never thinks to empty the dishwasher). This can cause some disharmony in the family.

3814–brings peace and a sense of satisfaction.

3936–has a lot of energy. You may have a business in the house, or perhaps you'll have a lot of guests. You may have parties or be the place where all the kids in the neighborhood gather. It can cause you to be helping others constantly, while forgetting to ask for something in return to balance the energy. If this is your tendency already, you should put a picture of your goal (new car, vacation destination, retirement piggy bank) on the wall near the front door, so you remember to take care of your needs before you hand the world everything you have.

4240–at its highest vibration and in the most positive light, this number 4240 reads as "through intense, structured effort you can tap into the essence of what you need and want." But energy, there's more of a desire to be right than happy. I suggest you display framed photographs of the family in the living room, dining room, and family room. This will symbolize the family united. Because this number's energy starts well, falters in the middle, and then ends well, it's important not to give up when things get rough. Perseverance leads to success.

41927–while the number does start on a FOUR, you'll be happy to know that it ends well. This number reads, although beginnings are difficult and require hard work, when the family gets into the flow of things, happiness and prosperity roll in. It's vital that the family be of one mind and not have arguments with each other. Even if there are differences of opinion, the family should agree to back each other up. Politics or religious differences can divide a house with this number. Also, this house may become a social place, a place where extended family or friends gather. The more social events, the more joy, and the more money opportunities.

83-5599-D–This is the longest number I've ever interpreted. This number means people realize dreams by making lots of adjustments and changes (and there will be hard work). Staying with a set plan can be a problem. Listening to people who think they know it all will cause difficulties. The way to prosperity and success lies in learning how to adjust and go with the flow. You may even need to break some rules.

there can be losses in a home with this house number despite hard work and care. A home with this energy benefits from having a home business with a product to sell (you need an inventory that reduces and sells out to prevent losses in other areas). A tax business would also be a profitable business for this home. Things in the home should be very organized, which could be quite challenging for a large family. But more people in the house, all going their separate directions, will help shift this energy to the positive.

4422–is a tough number. To shift this energy (if you want to stay in this home), have decor be modern with sharp angles and very clean surfaces. Have no clutter. Willingly let go of many things you no longer need. The more you let go of, the less loss you will experience. Choose colors that are dark, like gray and charcoal, to help mitigate the FOUR energy.

4704–has its challenges, but it also brings a gift. This number is about how we sometimes limit our prosperity and happiness because of rules we adopted long ago. This house amplifies those rules and helps you see them and judge whether the rules are valid and/or true. For example, a person might believe that mornings are difficult, making them late to work and holding them back in their careers. But in a 4704 house, they may find the sun brightly shines into their bedroom, helping them wake up early, and the sunshine gives them energy. Overall, this house will require a lot of work, but the gifts it brings (helping you break unhelpful rules that lock your prosperity potential) are worth it.

5029—gives an energy of sudden changes or disruptions followed by periods of absolute quiet. The family within the home can learn to grow and even benefit from this cycle. Many people don't like the ups and downs of life. They want things just to stay stable. But this never really happens in life; things always change. When a family needs the lesson that easy times are followed by stressful times, followed by easy times, they would fit well in this home. This home also works for people whose lives already follow this pattern (contract workers, temp workers, seasonal businesses, foster care homes, pet foster care, and so on).

5116—this number reads "independent people happily come together to form a family which results in hard work." To make life easier and mitigate the energy of hard work, it's important in this house not to have too much clutter. Get rid of stuff, and things will be better.

5225—has a mirror effect. So actions by one person reflect on others in the house. This house would bring a lot of change in your life.

5250—this house has a powerful social energy and could be a meeting place for friends and family. However, a house number that ends in ZERO can be a problem; there could be financial losses and disappointments. I would suggest you hang a wind chime on the back porch to call back opportunities and money that has been lost.

5605–is a home that brings a lot of change and opportunity, sometimes an overwhelming amount of change. If too many things seem to be happening at once, don't dig in your heels. Instead, know this is a good home and that everything will work out. Sometimes in this home, it will appear you're about to lose something or some opportunity, but it will be replaced by something even better. So if something goes away, just wait, something better is coming.

6338–is about nurturing ideas and creative opportunities that potentially can bring success and money. This house will be useful for writers, publishers, creatives, designers, and anyone who wants to build a business. This house will also help a couple have a stronger bond together if they share creative interests.

7053–can bring the temptation to give up and accept something less. The best use for this energy is to have an idea or a plan, allow the plan to fall apart, then rebuild with what's remaining. For example, you may think to add a second story to the home but find it structurally can't support the weight, so you instead build a small in-laws' quarters in the back yard. This energy will cause you to need to make compromises and adjustments.

7802–sometimes, houses that have a ZERO in the number need more home repairs. ZERO between numbers can also suck up money, and this creates debt. To catch money and keep it in the house, try placing a pretty bowl on a table near the center of the house. The bowl should be round (like a zero). The bowl can be empty or filled with round objects like coins or river stones.

10014–is about independent people coming together to work hard at something (a job, a project, a relationship.) Through loss or letting go, they can achieve family harmony and a steady income. This number is similar to 114; however, with the added zeros, there can be the potential for great creativity or, on the downside, long periods when nothing seems to be happening. This house would be best for people who have a business in the home, especially one that offers care to others (in some form). This house could also hold a lot of fertility energy. Try to avoid arguments in this home as the results could be a loss of the relationship.

10145–has the energy of independence being lost and then finding a new path through work and effort. This is a home where people grow spiritually and intellectually. But this number does have challenges, and so the home should be cleared regularly. It would be a good place for a social person with big ideas and lots of friends.

11925–is a stressful number. Everyone is independent and doing their own thing, and just when you think everything is going to work out, the unexpected happens, and everything changes. There is, however, a positive side to this number too. To bring financial success release old beliefs and look for new solutions. Add hanging crystals to catch the light and put rainbows on the walls representing a changing environment. They will also bring in new energy and opportunities for you and your family.

12478–this number shows everything increasing in your life, from your knowledge to your bank account. It can increase the size of your family through marriage or childbirth. The only negative is it can increase your waistline, so a healthy eating plan and exercise is essential in this home. This house adds up to a master number 22, which helps mitigate the FOUR root number energy. It says that if you design what you want in your future, you can manifest it. If you design small and ordinary, then that's what you'll get. If you design big, you will be amazed at what you can achieve. I suggest you write a list of wild and audacious goals for you and your family. Frame the list with a picture of your family in front of it (so the list is hidden from view) and place the picture in your living room or family room.

14308–this number reads as one person doing the work of several. At first, this brings little results, but in time it brings prosperity. You have to live in this house a while to get the full benefit. I suggest painting the ceilings bright white or hanging mobiles and chimes from the ceiling. This will lift you out of the drudgery and give you more success.

17221—means that individuals with strong opinions must unite into one common belief or goal. This will take hard work, and possibly there will be a loss (which could be one person giving up their dream to follow the other person's dream). If the person lives alone, the person may give up their dream to please their extended family.

19115—means that several like-minded people come together to share resources, and by combining their energy, they bring more to the household than they could have done separately.

21214—has the energy of a family trying to unify and come together as one. But some members of the household may be headstrong or want lots of independence. This can cause some difficulty in the house if the family is already prone to arguing. If the family members work at communication and show love to each other even while disagreeing, things will improve significantly in a year or so.

24647—is a very mixed energy of family togetherness and career focus. There are, unfortunately, some career challenges, unless your profession deals with communication, travel, politics, religion, education, or foreign countries. Any of these professions would improve in this energy.

34467—this number can bring a very successful career in communication, advertising, teaching, writing, and politics. However, it can also bring arguments within the family. With this

House Numbers for Investing in Real Estate

If you are buying a rental property or plan to fix up and flip your house, you want to pay attention to the house number. The number can have a literal effect on the price. Nicole Fortin, an Economics professor at the University of British Columbia, studied house sales. During a period from 2000 to 2005, he found that a house number EIGHT could fetch a 2.5% premium over other houses in the area. And a number FOUR house tends to sell for 2.2% less than comparable houses around it. The same goes for houses with the house number 13. According to the study, they also sell for 2.2% less than houses with another house number. This also goes for unit numbers of townhouses and condos. You'll have to work harder to make back your money with a unit that is a FOUR or 13.

When purchasing rental property, the house number will give you a clue as to what your tenants will be like.

ONE houses or apartments tend to attract independent people. They will be busy, tending to go from one project or job to another. They may not have time for yard maintenance, so you may want to tack on the charge for a gardener.

TWO houses or apartments bring people who are focused on relating and doing things together. Single people will find relationships, and this will cause them to either move the new love in or move out to find a place together. If a couple rents from you, they will enjoy the home.

THREE houses or apartments attract people who want to expand their family, individuals who are growing a business or studying. Tenants in these homes will communicate with you often and bring problems to your attention quickly.

FOUR houses or apartments attract people who are struggling either financially or personally. They will work hard, but there will always be a question of whether they can pull in enough income. The house or yard can become cluttered and unsightly. Sometimes even illness will come into the home and disrupt people's lives.

FIVE houses or apartments will bring people focused on social activities, parties, and playing games. There can be more breakage in homes like these, so you may want to set a higher deposit. Tenants can leave suddenly with little notice.

SIX houses or apartments tend to attract stable homebodies who want to decorate and make the place beautiful. Their family may expand while they live there, thereby adding a child, a pet, or having a relative come to live with them. They will become quite anxious if there's a delay in repair work; otherwise, they will be more careful maintaining the home.

SEVEN houses or apartments attract tenants who are students, teachers, or people who are studying something. People can be opinionated and argue in the home. They may sometimes be forgetful or not notice issues, and this can cause damage to the home (like not noticing a leaky pipe). When they're nice, they will be great tenants, and when they're not, they are most likely to sue.

EIGHT houses or apartments attract people who are looking for success. They may own a business and run it from home or may have some successful concern elsewhere. They will be interested in saving to get a house of their own, and they may speak to you about an option to buy the home.

NINE houses or apartments can bring people who want to stay a long time. They will be health-oriented. They may want to add décor touches of their own, like painting walls or removing wallpaper. They may collect a lot of furniture and things, but the home will be cozy and livable. Garages, attics, and basements, however, will be stuffed to the brim. And the tenants will seem like they are always working on decluttering the home.

A

ACKNOWLEDGMENTS

I want to thank Diane, Gary, Kelly, and ETC Publishing for their tireless work on my books. Their help and guidance made this book and the other books I write possible. Diane, we miss you very much.

About Donna Stellhorn

Donna has lived in houses, townhouses, and apartments of every root number. Her favorite numbers are THREE, EIGHT, and NINE. In a FOUR office, she built a business and then sold it for a tidy profit. In a house that was a FIVE, she renovated the house for a whole year, including rebuilding the staircase and raising the kitchen ceiling, as well as throwing fabulous parties. In the townhouse that was a NINE, she started her journey towards minimalism. Now she looks forward to each new house's energy, excited to see what opportunities it brings.

Donna Stellhorn is an Astrologer, Feng Shui expert, and has written 18 books, including Feng Shui Form and the best-selling booklet Sage & Smudge. Donna writes weekly and monthly predictions for Astrology.com and Horoscope.com. She offers a number of video courses, including Finding the Hidden Money in Your Chart and Tarot: Reading the Natural Way. Donna is a consulting Astrologer and sees clients every day. She is on the board of the NCGR–San Diego. For fun, Donna makes YouTube videos, and when she wants to be terrified, she does stand-up comedy. She lives in California, with the magical cat, LaRue.

website: https://donnastellhorn.com/

YouTube channel: https://www.youtube.com/c/DonnaStellhorn

One last thing...

Thank you so much for purchasing this book. I hope you found this information helpful, and if you did, please let your friends know about it. And if you can take a moment and review this book at your favorite bookseller, I would be very grateful.

Donna Stellhorn

Made in United States
Orlando, FL
11 December 2023

40690126R00088